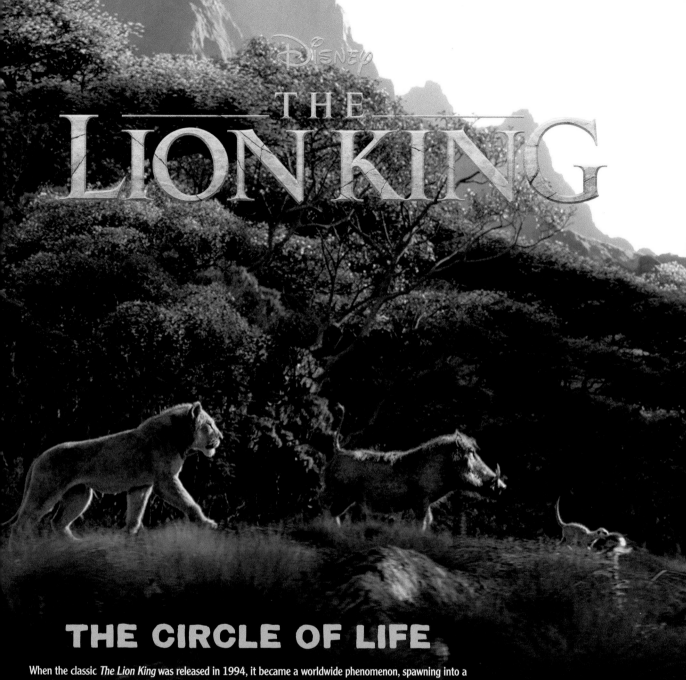

DISNEY THE LION KING

THE CIRCLE OF LIFE

When the classic *The Lion King* was released in 1994, it became a worldwide phenomenon, spawning into a groundbreaking stage musical, and now a whole new realization that combines techniques and vernaculars of animation, cinema, and human performance. Its characters and songs have captivated generations. Now, pioneering director Jon Favreau has reimagined *The Lion King* for a modern-day audience.

A revolutionary blend of virtual reality and new, ultrafast rendering technologies, *The Lion King* builds on the legacy of the original movie by bringing the adventures of its cast of iconic characters to stunning, vivid new life. In retelling the story of Simba, Nala, Mufasa, Scar, Timon, and Pumbaa, Favreau and his collaborators have reinvented the medium, crafting a film that points the way to the future for moviemaking and cinema. Twenty-five years on from its origins, the Circle of Life continues…

COLLECT THE OFFICIAL DISNEY SPECIALS

Dumbo
Toy Story 4
The Lion King
Frozen 2 (October 2019)
Artemis Fowl (May 2020)

DISNEY THE LION KING:
The Official Movie Special
ISBN: 9781787731820

DISTRIBUTION
US Newsstand: Total Publisher Services, Inc.
John Dziewiatkowski, 630-851-7683
US Newsstand Distribution: Curtis Circulation Company
US Bookstore Distribution: The News Group
US Direct Sales Market: Diamond Comic Distributors

For more info on advertising contact
adinfo@titanemail.com

Printed in the US by Quad.

Titan Authorized User. No part of this publication may be reproduced, stored in a retrival system, or transmitted, in any form or by any means, without the prior written permission of the publisher.

DISNEY PUBLISHING WORLDWIDE
Global Magazines, Comics and Partworks
Publisher: Lynn Waggoner. Editorial Team: Bianca Coletti (Director, Magazines), Guido Frazzini (Director, Comics), Stefano Ambrosio (Executive Editor, New IP), Carlotta Quattrocolo (Executive Editor), Camilla Vedove (Senior

Manager, Editorial Development), Behnoosh Khalili (Senior Editor), Julie Dorris (Senior Editor), Mina Riazi (Assistant Editor). Design: Enrico Soave (Senior Designer). Art: Ken Shue (VP, Global Art), Roberto Santillo (Creative Director), Marco Ghiglione (Creative Manager), Manny Mederos (Senior Illustration Manager), Stefano Attardi (Illustration Manager). Portfolio Management: Olivia Ciancarelli (Director). Business & Marketing: Mariantonietta Galla (Senior Manager, Franchise), Virpi Korhonen (Editorial Manager).

Thank you to Christopher Troise, Shiho Tilley, Eugene Paraszczuk and all at Disney. Also, Nick Jones.

TITAN

CONTENTS

Mufasa shows Simba his future kingdom, stretching as far as the eye can see (*Visual development artwork*)

THE STORY OF
THE LION KING

In the peaceful Pride Lands, the Circle of Life begins once more with the birth of a future lion king. On Pride Rock, Simba, the newborn lion cub of King Mufasa and Queen Sarabi, is presented by Rafiki, the king's shaman, to the assembled animals. Meanwhile, in the shadows, Mufasa's embittered brother, Scar, plots to usurp the king and dispose of Simba, with the aid of the hyenas Shenzi, Azizi, and Kamari. Simba and his lioness cub friend Nala have a near miss when they venture to the Elephant Graveyard (despite the protestations of Zazu, the king's hornbill majordomo). The pair avoid an early end thanks only to the timely intervention of Mufasa.

Then, engineered by Scar, tragedy strikes, sending Simba far from the Pride Lands to a new life in the Cloud Forest, where Timon the meerkat and Pumbaa the warthog give guidance in a new philosophy of life: "Hakuna Matata." But Simba's destiny as the rightful ruler of the Pride Lands cannot be denied, and in time he must return and take his place in the Circle of Life.

In his baobab tree, Rafiki daubs an image of the future Lion King (*Visual development artwork*)

JON FAVREAU

DIRECTOR

A pioneering film requires a fearless director. Enter Jon Favreau, who has spearheaded a groundbreaking new approach to moviemaking – using virtual cinematography and computer graphics techniques to craft a film of both legend and hyperrealism – in order to realize his vision of *The Lion King*.

01 Simba, the newborn lion cub and future king (*Rendered film frame*)

The Lion King – The Official Movie Special: **Were your experiences from directing The Jungle Book (2016) a help in approaching The Lion King?**

Jon Favreau: It took me the two and a half years of *The Jungle Book* to scale the learning curve. I came in as somebody who understood about visual effects from films like *Iron Man*, but this was going to be fully embracing CGI – not just a metal suit, but organic characters and fur. At the same time, while I'm learning more about how to use the technology effectively, the technology is getting better, so you're getting this synergistic confluence of circumstances that leads to the ability to show things on the screen in a way that you hadn't been able to before. What that does is it opens up the doors to being able to tell stories that otherwise would not have been possible.

Part of the fun of filmmaking is the innovation: pushing things technically and figuring out how to use new tools, and also creating tools that don't exist to help tell a story. I was very proud of how *The Jungle Book* came out, but I knew what was possible. So now I'm entering into *The Lion King*, inheriting all that I learned on *The Jungle Book*, and then seeing if we could take that next step, which was actually shooting an entire movie without any practical elements. The challenge with *The Lion King* was to do what was being presented as a live-action film, when in fact nothing is live action.

Why did you pick The Lion King as your next project after The Jungle Book?

I identified this as one that I felt I could really do something special with, because I understood how important that inherited relationship with the material and the characters and the music was. It has such powerful and timeless themes – not just musical themes, those as well, but I mean emotional themes, and themes that predate the film. You're dealing with archetypes and struggles that go back to *Hamlet* and before – all of the betrayal, coming of age, death and rebirth, and all of the cycles of life that are the foundation of all the myths around the

"THE CHALLENGE WITH *THE LION KING* WAS TO DO WHAT WAS BEING PRESENTED AS A LIVE-ACTION FILM, WHEN IN FACT NOTHING IS LIVE ACTION."

02

03

04

02 On Pride Rock, Simba is presented by Rafiki to the assembled animals (*Rendered film frame*)

03 Daubed in red, the newborn Simba is held aloft by Rafiki (*Rendered film frame*)

04 The Pride Lands in all their glory (*Concept artwork*)

world. Then bringing in the music from Africa, and the songs that Elton John and Hans Zimmer worked on, there was such a rich tradition surrounding this material. Now we had available to us a technology that could actually present these characters as if they were real, living animals, could we make it something that felt naturalistic, and beautiful, and real?

I had just been to Africa six months prior to when I was first talking about perhaps doing this film and discussing it with Disney. I was on safari with some people, and when a warthog ran by the safari vehicle, one of the people started singing "Hakuna Matata." Then, when we saw the lions up on a rock, they all said, "Look, it looks like *The Lion King*." It's become the frame of reference that everybody knows and accepts.

I've noticed how it pops up in comedy routines, in music, on TV shows, as part of sketches. It's constantly being referenced. It's such a deep part of our culture that it felt like there was a tremendous opportunity to do something to build on that, and to retell the story in a different medium. ▶

► **With the original film being so loved, were you at all daunted in creating this new version?**

Part of why we work so hard on the technology is because the case we have to make is: we're not reinventing the story, we're reinventing the medium. There was an acceptance going from the original film – which was a huge success in its day – to the stage production – and the musical was a huge success in its own right – of going from one medium to the other. Nobody ever felt that there was a redundancy between the two.

What we're hoping for and aspiring to here is to show this in a new way, and a new light, with a new style of filmmaking. Even though you're seeing a story you're familiar with and you're hearing songs you know – and it's a story that is following pretty closely what both of the other productions have done – it's going to feel new and not redundant, because we're going to present something totally new and exciting and magical through the techniques that we're using.

Did you discuss whether or not to introduce new characters, elements, or even new songs?

We explored it. Looking at animatics, sequences, and cuts with our story department, we'll always go to the original, and check it one last time. I have to say, quite often, the way the

> "WE USE VIRTUAL CAMERAS THAT ARE DRIVEN BY REAL EQUIPMENT AND A REAL FILM CREW, WHICH IS A UNIQUE CIRCUMSTANCE THAT I DON'T THINK HAS BEEN DONE BEFORE."

original movie did it was the right way to do it, and we ended up emulating that. So we definitely are not shy about going back to the old material, but it is amazing how much you can change and update invisibly. The trick is, you don't want it to feel like you've imposed yourself upon the film, but instead you want to pull out the best version of the film. Much like when productions are restaged, I'll make subtle edits to the material.

Of course, the big change, the big opportunity, is casting, because through casting we can bring another interpretation while still maintaining the spirit and the personality of the old film. That's where I think my contribution can be most seen, is me having a really good eye for who's going to fit into this thing well. I take a lot of pride in being able to see the talents of others, whether it's technical people behind the camera, or in front of the camera.

Are there particular shots that this new take on *The Lion King* recreates from the original?

It's not a shot-for-shot production, but there are sequences where everybody knows them really well that we stick closer to what was done. There are other areas where the story points are the same, but we'll allow ourselves to reinterpret and get there differently. So it's not like we're using the old script, and it's not like we're using the old shot list.

However, there are sequences where we either want to directly reference what was done before, or areas where we want to obliquely reference what was done. We never ignore what was done; it's always a choice to change it, update it. I think there are areas that age incredibly well, and there are others that feel a little bit of a different time. So, tonally, we update certain areas.

Also, the fact that everything looks live action and real creates a different set of challenges than doing a cartoon or a stage production. We have to figure out how not to cross the line of

05

06

making something feel too intense, of losing the thread of what we remember about the old film. Comedy works differently; music works differently; any sort of combat works differently. We're going for a PG movie here, which can be more intense than a children's film. It should feel like a family film, an adventure film, but there are areas where, even in the '94 film, even in the stage play, it feels very intense and emotional. So that's a balancing act that we approach differently, because we still want to hit those same feelings and the same story points, but we don't want to overwhelm the audience in a way that the other productions had not.

How organic is that process of updating?

What's nice about this is that the whole process is iterative. We'll start with script pages and drawings – our key frame art just for moments of the production – and Dave Lowry, our head of story, will start working with our story department and come up with show reels, story reels, animatics, like you would on an animated film.

Once we see that a sequence is working and moving right, then we transition over to building the environments digitally and creating them so that we can explore them in virtual reality. Andy Jones and the animators create simplified animated sequences that can run in real time in VR. Then we film in

"YOU HAVE THIS WONDERFUL INTERPLAY WHERE THE PEOPLE FROM A FILM BACKGROUND ARE LEARNING ABOUT THE TECHNICAL ASPECTS OF DIGITAL FILMMAKING, AND THEN YOU HAVE THE PEOPLE WITH THE DIGITAL BACKGROUND LEARNING THE AESTHETICS AND THE CULTURE OF MOVIES."

05 Simba lets out a mighty roar (*Rendered film frame*)

06 Scar and the hyenas make for a menacing sight (*Rendered film frame*)

VR. We use virtual cameras that are driven by real equipment and a real film crew, which is a unique circumstance that I don't think has been done before. We have a full film crew using digital tools in virtual reality.

Could you explain the virtual reality aspect a little more?

I think people of my generation who grew up with video games are very sensitive to photography and shots that look like they're completely digital. You could definitely tell the difference between a visual effect that was added to a real live-action plate, and one that was built completely in a computer. So the trick is, how do you make it look like it was really filmed? ▶

"YOU DON'T WANT IT TO FEEL LIKE YOU'VE IMPOSED YOURSELF UPON THE FILM, BUT INSTEAD YOU WANT TO PULL OUT THE BEST VERSION OF THE FILM."

► The way digital shots are designed is much more efficiently done. The camera move is designed ahead of time; the edit points and performance are all meticulous and perfect. But that perfection leads to a feeling that it's artificial. Not every generation of filmmaker is sensitive to this, but I find my peer group all have the same standard where we want it to feel like something that was actually photographed.

In the case of *The Jungle Book*, what was good was we had plates of real things that we would build the visual effects into, so we had the organic, practical nature of the photography that we were building off of. Here, we don't have that. In order to emulate that, we bring as much real human collaboration into the filmmaking process as you would in a live-action film.

Instead of designing a camera move on a computer, we lay dolly track down in the virtual environment; but that is being encoded by a dolly that exists, that has the same weight and characteristics of momentum and inertia that you would have in a real dolly. Even though the sensor is the size of a hockey puck, we build it onto a real dolly and a real dolly track. We have a real dolly grip pushing it, who is then interacting with Caleb Deschanel, our cinematographer, who is working real wheels that encode that data and move the camera in virtual space. So you'll see the same interplay that a camera and his dolly grip would have in designing a shot, because there are a lot of little idiosyncrasies that occur that you would never have the wherewithal to include in a digital shot. That goes for the crane work, and it goes for flying shots. We've also developed new rigs for this, like something that emulates a steadicam, and something that emulates a handheld by having the proper weighting and balance on this equipment.

07

08

How does this differ from other effects-heavy films?
Generally, what happens in the higher-tech films is, using motion capture technology they would motion capture the performances and then work the cameras in using essentially digital tools, because that gives you maximum freedom. Here, we're not capturing any of the performances, because it's all animals. Instead, we're capturing the camera movement.

We're putting all of our work into capturing the camera data and making the camera data feel like it's being driven by humans, and allowing the performances to be something that was inspired by human performance. But the humanity of those performances and the naturalism of those performances are coming from the artistry of the animators. Even in the way we scan environments in the sets, we're trying to bring as much reality into the set design as well.

Has this process informed your decisions as to who you picked as your heads of department?
We have a mixture of people from both the practical, traditional

09

07 Scar looms out
of the darkness of
his cave
(*Rendered film
frame*)

08 Simba and Nala,
both now fully grown,
reunite at the falls in
the Cloud Forest
(*Concept artwork*)

09 Fireflies flit
around wise Rafiki in
his baobab tree
(*Concept artwork*)

moviemaking world, and also people who are technical, like MPC [Moving Picture Company] and Magnopus. Depending on which position you're looking at, it'll either be somebody who's technically minded or somebody who has more of a cinema background. I find that that interface is what's creating the look of the movie.

When we started off, we had a full touch screen the size of a plasma monitor, and you could move assets around. You could move a rock or a tree, and anybody could walk over and do it, or anybody could pick up the camera and do it. One of the first things I decided was, that's not appealing to me. Part of how I make a film is by talking and scouting and collaborating with my department heads and crew members – people who know more about movies than I do. When I'm talking about photography and I have Caleb Deschanel there, I don't want to tell him what to do; I want to hear what he wants to do. I'm thinking about the big picture, but if he has a lighting technique or a camera move that he wants to do, I always want to hear what he has to say before I tell him what I want.

If a rock has to be moved on a screen, I don't want anybody to do it; I want my production designer and my art department to move it and move it back. I want to inherit the culture of filmmaking that's 100 years old. So you'll have [First Assistant Director] Dave Venghaus with a slider bar working a box to move the animals. If we need to offset a performance or puppet something, it'll work through him. When it comes to lighting, instead of having a gaffer, we have somebody who's working with the code and the programming who's helping to work the lighting, but Caleb is telling them where the sun should be.

You have this wonderful interplay where the people from a film background are learning about the technical aspects of digital filmmaking, and then you have the people with the ▶

BLACK BOX THEATER

Jon Favreau illuminates the black box theater technique – the unconventional method he and his team used to capture the performances of *The Lion King*'s voice actors.

"The reason that we used the black box theater technique was because I was trying to pursue an approach that made this film feel less like an animated movie and more like a live-action film. Instead of having people doing motion capture and getting that data, we were able to get the reference of the choices they were making from an acting perspective.

"Because most of these characters are lions, you can't just retarget a human performance captured from a face onto a lion and expect it to feel like a real lion. We would bring the actors into the room together and we made it a top-lit, dark little theater, like you would have for a theater rehearsal. Along the periphery on long lenses, we had video cameras that would be getting close-ups of all the actors.

"The big thing was to have this serve the purpose of a sound booth. Instead of giving their performances alone in a small sound booth, we soundproofed this room, so it allowed the actors to perform together. We had Caleb Deschanel out of the room watching monitors, making sure that he was getting what everyone needed.

"Once we got takes that we liked, we had the corresponding photography to ship off to our animators, and the animators were looking at reference footage. So you have a really interesting reference of a lion cub; then you have the actor performing; and then you have the storyboards and the animatics, and we have simple animation that's being done for the virtual reality stage. The animators work from all of those, and compile those to create a living, breathing performance.

"Using this technique, it allowed me to work with the actors as I would on a film set. I could talk to them; I could feed them ideas; I could have them pitch me an idea; I could have a writer or editor step in. So you're looking at it with the luxury of understanding the whole thing."

"I TAKE A LOT OF PRIDE IN BEING ABLE TO SEE THE TALENTS OF OTHERS, WHETHER IT'S TECHNICAL PEOPLE BEHIND THE CAMERA, OR IN FRONT OF THE CAMERA."

10 Young Simba
– about to face
his destiny

digital background learning the aesthetics and the culture of movies. What's exciting to me is that technology is often seen as something that's going to supplant what came before it, but in this case, we're extending the traditions of practical filmmaking into the digital age.

You're drawing on the very human input of your operators.

When we have everything going right, you inherit all of the idiosyncrasies of practical photography. In real photography, if you're into the nuance of it, when you're watching dailies you could tell which cameraman operates a shot. Certainly a cinematographer knows who did what. We want to inherit all of those happy accidents, all of those human idiosyncrasies.

In a medium that's so digital, that never actually goes through an analog phase – nothing's touching film, not even the release print – how do you infuse it with as much emotion and humanity as you can? Well, that comes from the humanity of the people operating the equipment. It comes from the human voices, the interpretations of the songs – Hans Zimmer and Pharrell Williams bringing their creative voices; real singers and real musicians coming together; people looking at animal reference and the animators breathing their life into these essentially digital, puppeted rigs. You're taking an incredibly antiseptic digital medium and telling one of the most emotional stories that we have in our tradition using these tools. To me, that dichotomy, that underlying tension creates a lot of creative opportunity.

It's a high-wire act. We really have to give it our all, because this is a big experiment, and people are very curious to see what we're doing. But I think that urgency, that sense of, if we do something really cool here, we can be affecting the way people make movies moving forward, is very exciting.

How does the VR stage work in practice? Is it real time?

The VR space is in real time. It could mean that we are cutting onstage because we have an editor onstage. Or if they're filming something, and I'm up in the editing suite, we have a feed, so I'm watching what's on camera. More often than not we will have planned what the work was, and I would have expressed what my priorities are; and sometimes there is a laundry list of shots; and sometimes there's exploration going on.

The most fun to me is seeing Caleb Deschanel, who's never been involved with anything technical to this extent, really embracing this set of tools and coming up with shots and techniques that I never even thought we'd be doing. He's surprised me with these inspired moments while still incorporating all of the elegance in his lighting and framing – which is the reason that I hired him and had been a fan. I never thought that I was hiring him because he was going to be innovative technically with these new tools, but in fact if you give a creative person a whole new paint set, they're going to do something interesting with it.

That's been fun, watching him and [Visual Effects Supervisor] Rob Legato collaborate – Rob, of course, is a cinematographer himself and a big fan of film and cinematography – and watching

> ## "THE PEOPLE WHO ARE MOST OFTEN DRAWN TO TECHNOLOGY ARE PEOPLE WHO ARE FIRST AND FOREMOST CONCERNED WITH PUSHING THE LIMITS OF TECH. BUT IN OUR CASE, WE WANT TO USE THIS TECHNOLOGY TO FURTHER HUMANIZE THE STORYTELLING."

the people from Magnopus react to what we want. They'll change the tool set and build and do a code dump, we'll go dark for a few days, come back, and we'll have a whole new set of tools.

For me, it's the best, because I like to walk around on a location scout in a real environment and say, "So the sun's going to be there? That's a nice background. So which side should they be on…? I guess if they come in from here…" You're talking with other people, and your production designer is saying, "I picked this location because I like that background," and the cinematographer will say, "Before lunch we should shoot this part of the scene and after lunch this part of the scene." Everybody's figuring out together how to do this.

So even with the VR stage, you and your team are tapping into the classic language of filmmaking.

There is what you would really see with the naked eye, and there's what you would see in a movie, and often what you would see in a movie feels more real than what you would see with the naked eye.

We have to make decisions about how you show stars: this movie has monologues about the stars in the sky, and we have to show stars. Now, if you take a real film camera and you film a sky, you don't see stars. When you walk outside and you look up in the sky, you have a much greater range of light levels you can see; you could be talking to your friends, and you could see the stars. But in a movie, if you put stars in, it would look fake, it would look digital. So what do we do? We look at old movies that showed stars. How did they do it for *Close Encounters of the Third Kind*? The way they comped the stars in in *Close Encounters* is artificial, but because we have accepted that growing up watching it, we'll often emulate what a movie would have done and not what real life presents you with.

These are the discussions I love having with Rob and with Caleb. Rob has been involved in recent times with some classic, classic productions, but he's a fan of films of the '70s. Then with Caleb, he was really making those movies; he was there shooting inserts on *The Godfather* and on *Apocalypse Now*. So it's a tremendous resource, and it's great to have the different generations of filmmakers come together. Because my sensibility is very different from Rob's, which is very different from Caleb's, as we come together and develop a shared sensibility, that's when the voice of the film comes through.

That's why to me the collaboration of humans is the most important part of this incredibly technical and technological film. The people who are most often drawn to technology are people who are first and foremost concerned with pushing the limits of tech. But in our case, we want to use this technology to further humanize the storytelling.

THE VOICES OF THE PRIDE LANDS

01 James Earl Jones reprises his role of Mufasa from the classic *The Lion King* movie for the 2019 version

02 Director Jon Favreau talks Donald Glover through a scene

03 & 04 Billy Eichner and Seth Rogen record their Timon and Pumbaa roles, respectively

05 Donald Glover voices his Simba role

06 Chiwetel Ejiofor focuses for his Scar role

05

06

JON FAVREAU ON
MUFASA
JAMES EARL JONES

asting starts with being nervous! Especially in the case of this movie. What do you do? A lot of the original cast are still around; what messages are you sending with each announcement?

"What we wanted to do was honor the past, but also look forward and do something fresh. That's why the first two announcements that we made – I wanted to make sure they were at the same time – were James Earl Jones coming back as Mufasa, and then Donald Glover playing Simba.

"I think the audiences who were paying attention – the people out there who are tapped into social media, who had an ear to the ground on this production – overwhelmingly supported what we were doing. With a new production, you want somebody to bring their own version to it. It's a cover

band, not a tribute band, so you want somebody to bring their own thing to it. Now, sometimes you want to hear the exact same solo lick as the song that you knew; but sometimes you just want to capture the spirit of it. When you can capture the spirit but show the audience something new and surprising, that's the best combo.

"In the case of Mufasa and James Earl Jones, that was the one role which was so timeless in the themes that his character dealt with, so anything that we were rewriting, or anybody else we were picturing as Mufasa, was not as good as what was there. But it's been 25 years since the last production. It's still the same guy, but it's a slightly different take on Mufasa; it was a different point in his life. The areas where it was more colloquial or there was more humor, that's where there was room for reinvention, just as you would in a stage play."

02

01 Master of all he surveys, Mufasa stands atop the iconic Pride Rock with his son, Simba
(*Visual development artwor*

02 The King of the Pride Lands is a wise and noble ruler
(*Visual development artwor*

03 A tender moment between Mufasa and young Simba
(*Visual development artwor*

01

"WE WANTED TO HONOR THE PAST, BUT ALSO LOOK FORWARD AND DO SOMETHING FRESH."

JAMES EARL JONES
Selected Credits

FILMS

Rogue One, 2016
Darth Vader

Driving Miss Daisy, 2014
Hoke

Cry, the Beloved Country, 1995
Rev. Stephen Kumalo

The Hunt for Red October, 1990
Admiral Greer

Field of Dreams, 1989
Terence Mann

Coming to America, 1988
King Jaffe Joffer

Return of the Jedi, 1983
Darth Vader

Conan the Barbarian, 1982
Thulsa Doom

The Empire Strike Back, 1980
Darth Vader, uncredited

Star Wars, 1977
Darth Vader, uncredited

TV

3rd Rock from the Sun, 1996
Narrator

Star Wars Rebels, 2014-2016
Darth Vader

Paris, 1979-1980
Detective Captain Woody Paris

03

DONALD GLOVER

SIMBA

Actor, comedian, writer, producer, director, musician: Donald Glover has done it all. All, that is, except playing a lion... until now. In Disney's reimagined *The Lion King*, the renaissance man channels his talents and love for the 1994 original into a unique new take on Simba.

01 A majestic Simba on the prowl (*Concept artwork*)

T

he Lion King – The Official Movie Special: How does it feel to be part of this new version of The Lion King?
Donald Glover: It's very special. I have a son who loves animals, and the lion is his favorite, so it will be cool that in two years he'll be old enough to understand. He's really going to love this. I actually feel a great amount of responsibility. I didn't feel the joy of it immediately, I felt all the responsibility, because I know how much it meant to me, and now it will be out there forever.

What did you think when you first heard about the project?
When I first heard Jon Favreau was doing it, I was very excited, because I really liked *The Jungle Book* adaptation he did. He has a good knack for updating things without changing them. I think that's really hard to do. Most people hate sequels. I understand: I'm one of those people. It's not that I don't like change, but I don't like it when things don't have a voice, and sometimes the voice that's in it already is enough. But he really cares about the project and really wants to speak to it. I think the message that this movie has is extremely relevant.

How did you become involved with the film?
I met Jon before a *Hollywood Reporter* roundtable that we were doing. We shook hands, and we talked, and he said his son was a fan of my music, and I said, "Thank you, that's very cool." We just talked and hung out. We did the roundtable, and then afterwards an assistant said, "Jon wants to talk to you for a moment." I thought I must have said something stupid at the table, like "*Iron Man* wasn't that great" or something like that. Jon took me to the side and said, "I don't know if you've heard, but I'm making *The Lion King*." I said, "Oh, yeah, congratulations." He said, "Do you want to be Simba?" It was like that. I thought that stuff goes through agents, or you get a call or something monumentous, but it was just, "I'm doing this thing; you want to play too?" I was really grateful for the opportunity.

02

02 Looking into the water, Simba sees his father's face reflected in his own (*Concept artwork*)

03 Simba finds a new family (*Rendered film frame*)

04 Mufasa shows young Simba his kingdom (*Rendered film frame*)

05 Simba faces a challenge to the throne in the form of his uncle, Scar (*Concept artwork*)

What was your research for the role of Simba?
I watch animal shows all the time anyway, and I watched them in the studio when I was recording just for fun, because *Animal Planet* and *Planet Earth* and all those shows are the most honest things on television. They're not edited really; you just see honest things. I guess that was the most research. As far as watching the original movie, I did watch it with my son just to watch it again, but I knew it so well already. Me and my brother and sister probably watched it every Saturday for at least a year [when we were young].

What is it about The Lion King story that resonates, do you think?
It's a very human and honest story of what everything goes

03

04

05

"SIMBA WANTS TO IMPRESS MUFASA, AND MUFASA IS TRYING TO GET HIM TO UNDERSTAND THAT THAT'S NOT WHAT LIFE IS [ABOUT]."

through. Nothing is permanent. It's such a great and beautiful way of showing – even to children – how permanence is not the point, more is not the point; the point is to be here and to be responsible for each other and love each other. There's always going to be change, and there will always be each other, so why are we not helping each other? I think that's very special.

How did you approach the character of Simba?

The way I went about it was, even with the voice direction – little things and inflections – I was trying to show that Simba is still a child until he confronts what happened to him.

Do you personally relate to Simba?

Absolutely. I feel very, very connected to Simba's journey. I

feel like a kid most of the time, and I think that's because the world is a very scary place to me. I grew up on *Sesame Street* and Disney, where people are nice because that's what you're supposed to do. But the world's not really like that. So you have to balance yourself and hopefully pass on good things to your children and the people around you.

What is Simba's predicament initially?

Simba is the prince, and his father, Mufasa, is the king. Something horrible happens when Mufasa dies at the hands of his brother, Scar, although Simba's not sure of it at that time. Scar tells Simba to run away and not to come back so he can take his place. Simba's whole journey is really deciding, "Am I going to face this? Or am I just going to run away forever?" That's the sad part: some people sometimes do run away forever, because it's too painful to go back.

How would you characterize Simba's uncle, Scar?

Scar has a real taste for the throne. He really wants to be king; he thinks he'd be a better king than Mufasa, and wants to make an alliance with the hyenas, which I guess sounds good in one respect. But if you're not really thinking about the circle of life and how things work and how we all help each other, it's more of a conquest rather than a balance. Chiwetel Ejiofor does an amazing job of being a devious lion. He has quite the presence and recording with him was very helpful.

Can you define Simba's relationship with his father?

I think Simba and Mufasa's relationship is standard in the sense that Simba wants to impress Mufasa, and Mufasa is trying to get him to understand that that's not what life is. It's not about who's going to be the best; it's about playing your role and doing what you're supposed to do, which means responsibility. ▶

DONALD GLOVER
Selected Credits

FILMS

Guava Island, 2019
Deni Maroon

Solo: A Star Wars Story, 2018
Lando Calrissian

Spider-Man: Homecoming, 2017
Aaron Davis

The Martian, 2015
Rich Purnell

The Lazarus Effect, 2015
Niko

TV

Atlanta, 2016-
Earnest "Earn" Marks

Adventure Time, 2013-2016
Marshall Lee

Community, 2009-2014
Troy Barnes

Girls, 2013
Sandy

30 Rock, 2006-2012
various

Bronx World Travelers, 2007
Scoopy Brown

Human Giant, 2007
Mitchell the Webcam Guy

It's hard to teach a child responsibility, and especially as a king, because you have a lot of responsibility. When Mufasa tells Simba, "All of this will be yours, everything the light touches," it sounds like, "Yeah, I'm going to own all that!" When it's really, "No, you have to protect all of this." Having James Earl Jones say those things to you is very moving. He feels like the dad reminding you of your responsibility of just being alive. It's really beautiful.

What's Simba's take on Timon and Pumbaa?
Simba's take on Timon and Pumbaa is that these guys are cool; they like him when no one really should like him, and they help him through something very traumatic. Seth and Billy do a really good job playing these two vagabond outcast guys.

What was it like recording "Hakuna Matata" with Seth Rogen and Billy Eichner?
Really funny. They're very funny guys, obviously, but it was cool, because we all know these songs really well, and they added something brand-new and lifelike in them, which I really loved.

What was the dynamic like when you were recording?
Pretty much just us cracking jokes on each other. We were all in a room in a triangle, sitting there, and there were cameras and stuff, so any mess-ups were just met with laughter. It was really fun, because we knew it a lot, so there was a lot more improv. No one was really afraid to improv because everybody knew the script already.

How did you find the recording process?
I like to be able to self-edit, to be quite honest. I like being able to do it again. When you're acting, it's different: you're in the moment, and you're not able to see it. When you're

06

"I FEEL VERY CONNECTED TO SIMBA'S JOURNEY. I FEEL LIKE A KID MOST OF THE TIME, AND I THINK THAT'S BECAUSE THE WORLD IS A VERY SCARY PLACE TO ME."

07

JON FAVREAU ON
DONALD GLOVER

"Donald Glover is an amazing singer, and also an amazing improviser, which is one of the things that really drew me towards him, because he comes from a similar comedic background to me. He came up with a lot of the people that I came up with; I was in the Chicago improv scene, which overlaps with [comedy collective] Upright Citizens Brigade and Tina Fey's world and all that. So I knew that we were going to have a common take on how to do comedy and how to do that type of performance. He's since come into his own, of course, as Lando Calrissian, and working on a lot of projects such as *Atlanta*, so I thought a guy who has talents in all those areas was going to bring a lot of dynamism to the part, and charm, and a wonderful voice, and a really great attitude about the way he could creatively engage, and the way audiences react to him. It felt just right."

How would you describe the relationship between Simba and Nala?

They're best friends who slowly realize they have more in common. I guess that's a classic thing of a partnership, of knowing you're really good friends and growing into somebody you trust. She's the only person who is able to get through to him in a really hard and dark time in his life.

What makes Simba ultimately decide to go back home to the Pride Lands?

I think Nala speaking to him, and him recognizing his father in himself through Rafiki, is really what drives him to go back – knowing that life is responsibility, not just to everybody else or the Pride Lands, but to yourself. Being told you are the rightful king, that's what you're here for.

How has it been to get a glimpse of this revolutionary new version of *The Lion King* being made?

This has been a really incredible experience. I've never seen anything made this way before. I don't think there has been anything made this way before, so getting to hang out and see how things are made is really great. The animators are so talented. Just on a technical level, getting to see how they're doing this – the stage and the camera work and the drawings and the animatics – I feel blessed to be a part of it. It really does feel unreal.

Did you get to fully immerse yourself in the virtual-reality aspect of the project?

I did the whole thing. I put on the VR; I got to set up a camera during the stampede; I got to see that whole scene where he falls into the stampede from any angle I wanted; I got to hover above: it was incredible. It was like lucid dreaming. It really is industry-changing.

What are you most excited for the audience to discover?

Honestly, I am most excited for them to have the same feeling I had when I saw *The Jungle Book*, which was the same story, but not the same story. I really am excited for that with this movie. It's just beautiful-looking; the level of detail and love in all the characters, and the hairs and the faces and the eyes and the noses and the way the flamingos' heads are moving. It's hard to make a movie like this and have that level of care where everybody knows how much it means and everybody's that invested, so it's a special moment. It's mind-blowing. 🦁

recording, you're seeing pictures and animatics and you're really breathing life into them. You're emoting with really just your voice, and I think that's fun, because you can go anywhere you want, and you know that's what they're using to make these characters. If you do it really loud or fast, or emote really hard, that's how they'll draw it. So you need to really give it to them vocally so they can capture it, which is really special.

Is it easier to record alone or with other actors?

I prefer to have someone in there with me. Doing it by yourself is great, and it's fun, especially with a movie that is as iconic as *The Lion King* because you know all the parts. But it was so nice to have Chiwetel and Seth and Billy right in front of me, because you get stuff that you wouldn't expect.

What was your initial reaction to Beyoncé being on board as Nala?

I guess my reaction was, "Does she know I'm Simba…?" It was funny. A lot of my friends were like, "You get to kiss Beyoncé. Does Jay-Z know that you get to kiss Beyoncé?" I was like, "It's a cartoon, so we're not really kissing. At most I'll get to make kiss sounds, but I don't know if that's how lions do it."

06 A grown-up Simba surveys his kingdom from Pride Rock (*Concept artwork*)

07 Nala and Simba's childhood friendship eventually turns to love (*Concept artwork*)

"THIS HAS BEEN AN INCREDIBLE EXPERIENCE. I'VE NEVER SEEN ANYTHING MADE THIS WAY BEFORE. I DON'T THINK THERE HAS BEEN ANYTHING MADE THIS WAY BEFORE."

JON FAVREAU ON
NALA
BEYONCÉ KNOWLES-CARTER

"For the older version of Nala, we have Beyoncé. When you think of somebody who you'd be excited to hear reinterpret this role, especially the musical performances, she's in a class all by herself. When you have tweens and teens at home, it's a struggle to remain cool because you're irritating to your children, but having Beyoncé in my film definitely bought me a lot of credibility on campus with my kids and their friends.

"I'm very excited and a big fan of her music. She's very down to earth, friendly, and was excited to be working on this. She has kids of her own, so the fact that she was working on *The Lion King* was something that she could share with her family, and they're very excited about it too.

"I find that in making these movies, part of what's so fun about it is that the filming process, the planning process, casting, screenings, and promotion; it's something that I do with my family. That's been a really fun aspect of this, and the people that we collaborate with find that, too. It's something you don't necessarily realize when you're starting, but through the process of it, you realize that it's something you can share with them. Often, work draws you apart from your family, and here there are opportunities for you to have shared experiences that are really fun. Also, the kids have very strong opinions. I've made a lot of good decisions on my collaborations on these family films because I've listened to my family – and they definitely are not shy in telling me what they think about what I'm planning to do."

BEYONCÉ
Selected Credits

<u>FILMS</u>
Epic, 2013
Queen Tara
Obsessed, 2009
Sharon
Cadillac Records, 2008
Etta James
Dreamgirls, 2006
Deena Jones
The Pink Panther, 2006
Xania
The Fighting Temptations, 2003
Lilly
Austin Powers in Goldmember, 2002
Foxxy Cleopatra

<u>TV</u>
Homecoming, 2019
(Director and subject of documentary)
Wow! Wow! Wubbzy!, 2009
Shine

01 A grown-up Nala and Simba rekindle their friendship (*Visual development artwork*)
02 Nala grows from a curious cub into a strong and noble lioness (*Visual development artwork*)

"HAVING BEYONCÉ IN MY FILM DEFINITELY BOUGHT ME A LOT OF CREDIBILITY WITH MY KIDS AND THEIR FRIENDS."

CHIWETEL EJIOFOR

SCAR

To play Scar, the embittered brother of King Mufasa, British actor Chiwetel Ejiofor brought to bear his background in Shakespeare in order to tap into the duplicity and tragedy of the character. He also had to become accustomed to channeling his interpretation of Scar solely through his voice, something the star found challenging, but ultimately rewarding.

01 No longer a cub, Simba is ready to challenge his scheming uncle for the throne (*Concept artwork*)

The *Lion King – The Official Movie Special:* **What is it about this story that resonates so much with audiences?**
Chiwetel Ejiofor: The story is so epic. It has these great arcs, it has great heroes, great villains, and a great compass – a real sense of social consciousness and a moral idea at the heart of it. So it's very appealing and informative, as well as entertaining. These characters take you on extraordinary, emotional, very complicated journeys, so bringing them back in a way that can actually be, in some ways, more relatable, where you can really fall down the rabbit hole with these characters, is pretty stunning.

How would you describe Scar, your character?

Scar is a very complicated, malevolent character, and therefore fun to play. Scar works as a bad guy because there's nothing mundane about him. He doesn't want anything as everyday as revenge; he's not fighting for small things. He wants power. He wants it all, and there's nothing that he won't do to get it. He's an incredible character in that way. He'll push all of the boundaries. He'll do absolutely anything and everything to get what he wants, and he's written with a slyness – almost a little twinkle – that is incredibly interesting and fun to step into.

What kind of research did you do for the role?

I was very familiar with the film, the show, and the epic, Shakespearean quality of the character; [with the] Hamlet-like nature of the relationship with the father, and the brother being killed. All of those elements were there. So that, in a way, was the research for the character, if you could even call it that. Research makes it sound like work, and it wasn't. It was such a fun part to explore, and such an amazing history and film and characters – and in this context, drawn on this scale, it's very exciting.

02 Scar's thirst for power leads to a dramatic showdown above the canyon (*Concept artwork*)

03 Scar's treachery prevails, resulting in the death of the noble Mufasa (*Concept artwork*)

"SCAR'S RELATIONSHIP WITH SIMBA IS ONE THAT'S FOUNDED ON JEALOUSIES."

02

03

What is the relationship between Scar and his brother Mufasa, the King?

Generally in a pack of lions there'll only be one lion, so on the rare occasions that there are two, one is pushed into the shadows. That's where Scar is. It's a relationship built on jealousy and being pushed into the corners, and the mistakes that Scar has made in the life he lived before he was Scar. So this relationship is one that's fraught with all those difficulties. With the arrival of Simba, he realizes that he'll never get what he really wants, which is to be king, to be all-powerful, and that tips him over the edge. He sets in motion a chain of events to take control.

How about the relationship between Scar and Simba? How would you characterize that?

Again, it's a very complicated relationship between Scar and Simba, and of course it's the area in which Scar shows himself to be the most heartless and malevolent: the trick of convincing Simba that he's responsible for his own father's death is at the heart of the nature of this very scheming character.

As with Mufasa, his relationship with Simba is one that's founded on jealousies. I think Scar is envious of that whole set-up between the father and son; of the way they are together, of what they represent together, and what he can't access. That really strong bond of love and righteousness that they exude; he can't access it in his life, so he attempts to exploit it and destroy it, which again is very deeply rooted in the epic tales and in Shakespearean literature – the corruptibility of love is a massive theme in Shakespeare.

So here again is this bond that is exploited for Scar's gains. It's a very interesting and complex relationship he has with Simba, but it's also playful in its own malevolent way. He's very playful with the young cub, even as he's doing these very dastardly things.

What effect does Scar ultimately have on the Pride Lands?

It's interesting that once he gets control of the Pride Lands, they fall apart. It's almost power for the sake of power – not to do much with it, not to progress things, just to get there. Power for power's sake is a real condition, and also, by the nature of the thing, once he has what he perceives to be in any way a victory, then it's hollow. He's not aware of what he's really fighting for, because he can't ever gain that inner peace; there's no amount of power that will restore him to what he ▶

04

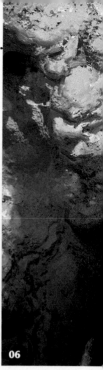

06

04 As a cub, Simba is unaware of his uncle's villainy
(*Concept artwork*)

05 Scar's jealousy has driven him to become an outcast
(*Concept artwork*)

06 Mufasa and Scar - brothers at war
(*Concept artwork*)

07 Pride Rock is the setting for Simba and Scar's dramatic showdown
(*Concept artwork*)

▶ believes to be his rightful place, because it doesn't really exist.

All of this is an outward projection of what he thinks he wants, what he thinks he needs. Then, when he gets it, he realizes that it's not enough, and so he doesn't do much with it. The place starts to fall apart, it all gets destroyed, and so then there's a need for redemption, which is inevitably going to happen. When it does, he almost meets that with a resignation and understanding that it's the circle of life, and that things will be restored to what they were – and they have to be.

What is Scar's dynamic with the hyenas?

In the 1994 film, Scar's relationship with the hyenas is quite light – there's a levity to it. In this, we're reaching a little bit further into the malevolence of all of these characters and this situation. It becomes more rooted and grounded in reality within this context. That's interesting. It creates a certain mood. I think the whole piece has a certain mood, and there are real stakes. When it's scary, it's scary; when it's engaging, it's engaging, and so that gives you this play and relief when things move back to where they could naturally be. I think that balance is very important; that sense that the stakes are very high. Once you play and hit into those slightly darker, more malevolent tones, it's a really nail-biting piece.

05

What is it like to see the visual representation of your character?

Seeing Scar come to life – and that is very literally what it feels like, just seeing this character arriving fully formed, living, breathing, snarling – is very powerful. It's true for all of the characters. The way that it's brought to life really puts you into that world, but it's also a world that you want to be in, that you want to sit in and observe and spend some time in and wander around in. It makes you want to get down there and check out other things, and then be told the story. It's very exciting; it's a really beautiful move in this landscape, and I think it'll be very, very engaging for an audience.

How did you find the recording process?

You can't rely on any ticks, gestures, hands, eyes; your vocal quality is going to be the only thing really that communicates the character, until the character becomes fleshed out. Then, of course, there's a whole other stream of work that uses your voice as the bedrock and then builds the character around it. But during the early stages, you're really trying to give the vocal quality all of the fullness that you can – because at that point, that's really communicating the whole character. It was a challenge.

Was it helpful getting to record with some of the other actors, rather than just on your own?

When people are there, you can really play off somebody else. It elevates the whole piece, and you really do get a sense of being in situ with great actors and great performances. Naturally, having somebody to bounce off really changes things and lifts them. With both Donald [Glover] and Florence [Kasumba], it's having people who are brilliant actors, who can really embody characters, who are really brave and prepared to go there and do all the things, and that becomes very exciting. Scar has most of his interactions with their two characters, so I was very, very lucky to meet and work with them both.

How was working with Jon Favreau?

Jon seems to have it all in his head. He understands every

JON FAVREAU ON
CHIWETEL EJIOFOR

"Scar is played by Chiwetel Ejiofor, who is just a wonderful actor who brings his British accent and, I think, a bit of the Shakespearean cadence to [the role]. He brings a new take on that character. Jeremy Irons did a fantastic job [in the 1994 original], the character is a very scary villain; and with Chiwetel you have someone who's doing something different but still evocative of the old version of Scar. Because of his background as an actor, he brings the feeling of a Shakespearean villain to bear.

"It's wonderful when you have somebody as experienced and seasoned as Chiwetel. Through his voice he breathes such wonderful life into this character. He's somebody who you could take away a lot of their other tools – like their face, the way their body moves – and it all comes through their voice. I knew we were going to be in very good shape with him."

"SCAR IS A VERY COMPLICATED, MALEVOLENT CHARACTER, AND THEREFORE FUN TO PLAY."

part of the journey – the epic nature of the story, the animation, and the overall look and feel and texture of the film. It is really impressive how he holds that all together, and seemingly with ease. I know there's sweat behind there somewhere, but I can't see it yet.

Also, being an actor as well, he understands how to work with actors, how to get the best out of them, and how to support them, especially as some of this is slightly newer territory for me. He's somebody who's really very aware of that, and very sensitive to it, and can guide you through all the choices and the ranges of it so you can find the character, find that performance, and find how you tell the story.

What are you most excited for audiences to discover?
I love the idea of audiences rediscovering something. That's what gave me goosebumps when I saw the first bits of footage of this: you remember and recall all of the excitement of the story. You know that it's going to be very compelling and exciting, but this is taking it to another stage, taking it further and deeper. There's a roundness to it that I think is going to be very compelling – the way the world has been created, and how these animals are going to look telling this very epic story, with its great highs and plunging lows, and then its redemption. It's moving, and it's engaging, and it's fun, and funny at times, and a really great story. 🦁

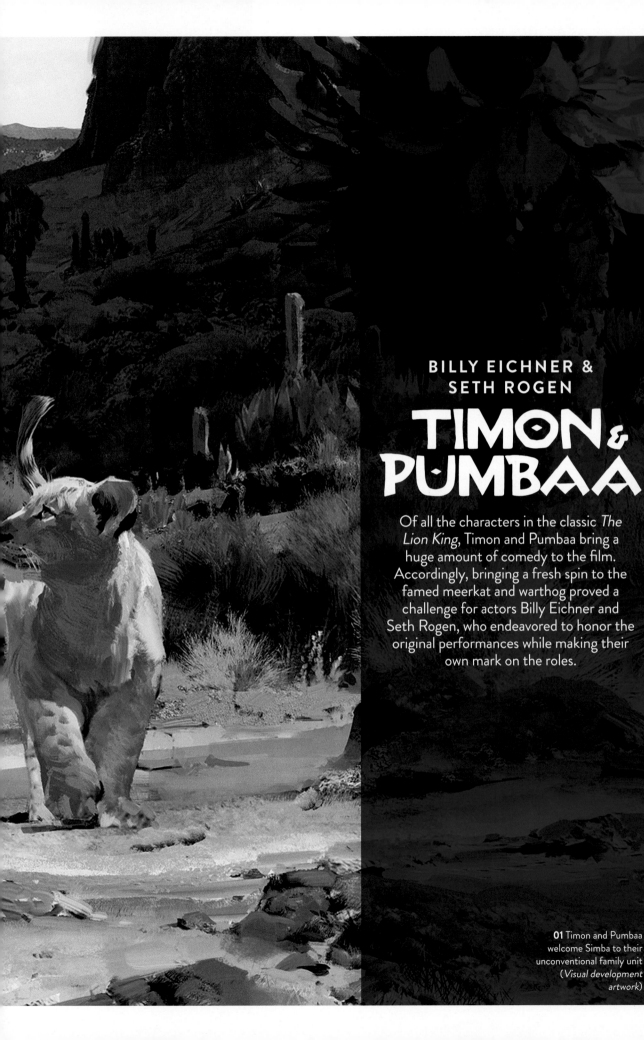

BILLY EICHNER &
SETH ROGEN

TIMON & PUMBAA

Of all the characters in the classic *The Lion King*, Timon and Pumbaa bring a huge amount of comedy to the film. Accordingly, bringing a fresh spin to the famed meerkat and warthog proved a challenge for actors Billy Eichner and Seth Rogen, who endeavored to honor the original performances while making their own mark on the roles.

01 Timon and Pumbaa welcome Simba to their unconventional family unit (*Visual development artwork*)

The Lion King – The Official Movie Special: Seth, you've known Jon Favreau for close to two decades; how did he contact you about the role of Pumbaa?

Seth Rogen: He just emailed and said, "Would you like to be Pumbaa?" I was like, "Absolutely." I was a little surprised, but honestly, in the back of my head I was secretly hoping that I would get the part.

I was a huge fan of the original movie. I grew up with it – I've seen it so many times – so it's a little hard at first to separate yourself from it and to not organically do the thing that the other person's done. But it became clear pretty early on that there would be ways to create a new dynamic between the characters.

Billy, what do you think makes *The Lion King* so iconic?

Billy Eichner: What can you say about it? It's *The Lion King*, this legendary, epic, classic movie! I'm a huge Disney fan – I go to Disneyland all the time – so to get the call to be a part of that legacy is really shocking and thrilling.

Did you do any research for your role of Timon?

BE: I've been living as a meerkat for about four years now. But I still kept my phone…

I purposely have not gone back to watch the original movie. I did go see the Broadway show recently with Jon Favreau – he was in New York and invited me; what was I going to do, say no? But I did not revisit the original movie version. So much of it was still in my head, because those are such iconic songs, and the whole movie is so iconic. I thought it was in my head enough already that it would make it a bit harder to put my spin

02 Under Timon and Pumbaa's tutelage, Simba grows from cub to proud young lion (*Visual development artwork*)

03 "Hakuna Matata" – Simba learns an important life lesson and puts his past worries behind him (*Visual development artwork*)

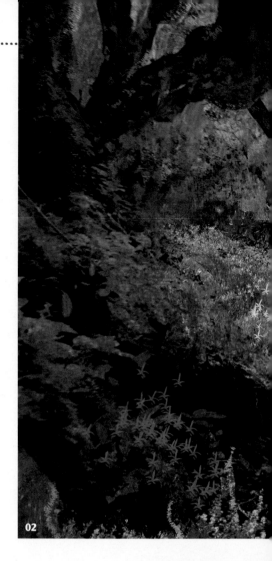

02

03

on it with Nathan Lane's [Timon] voice constantly echoing in my ear. What he did was so perfect and so funny. I don't think you can be better.

All I can hope is that I honor what he did and add a little bit of new flavor to it: some new jokes here and there, and make it a bit more me. I'm not as good as Nathan Lane, but I grew up loving him and larger-than-life performers like him – and I do come from that school as well, I think.

Do you relate to the character of Timon at all?

BE: There's a lot of crossover there. Timon is a bit of a showman – at least, I'm playing him that way. I think Timon likes to be the center of attention. I'm a pretty big person in real life, and Timon is small, but he behaves like a big person, and he has a big personality. There's a great sense of entitlement; he's very quick to make himself the center of attention, and then also let you know how exhausted he is by all of it. I'm playing around with that a lot. I relate to him – his sarcasm, his energy. He has a lot of personality, and I relate to that.

Seth, did Jon talk to you about the singing aspect of the film before you signed on?

SR: I didn't know what his take was, so I didn't know if all the songs from the original were going to be in this. Then they told me that they were, and I was like, "I can't sing." I probably dance better than I sing, and that's not very well. I'm honestly tone deaf. I can't discern which notes I'm singing. It just is a fluke. It's

like the monkeys and typewriters theory: if I just sing enough, odds are one of the times the right notes will come out of my mouth. That's my approach: do it 200,000 times and one of those is probably good.

Does it help having Hans Zimmer and Pharrell Williams working on the music?

SR: No – it's much more intimidating when it's the most famous, skilled people. It'd be like if you couldn't ice skate for a movie, and they got Wayne Gretzky [former professional ice hockey player] to help you. I would be much happier if it was just some vocal coach named Jim who lived in Studio City. That would've been much less intimidating.

Billy, what was it like to be in a room filled with such talent?

BE: It's pretty remarkable. When we were recording "Hakuna Matata," it was me, Seth Rogen, Donald Glover, Hans Zimmer, and Jon Favreau, in addition to an amazing crew of people working on it in the recording studio. It was surreal. Seth was looking at me, we were all looking at each other, like, "We're doing *The Lion King*? Are you sure?" It's pretty wild.

At the same time, you have to ignore the legacy to a certain degree. You can't let it get into your head, because it would be too intimidating, so you've got to dive in there and trust your instincts and make it your own. ▶

04

Seth, how have you found working with Billy?

SR: I've known Billy for years. I'm a big fan of his show, *Billy on the Street*, [which] I've been on.

On this film, we got to work together in this kind of theater with JD [McCrary], who is little Simba, and Donald [Glover, adult Simba]. To be with other people was helpful, and very unconventional. I've done a lot of voiceover stuff, but very few things I've done you're actually with the person, and none of them [involve] acting it out in a theater. Just to be able to stand up and act it out with the other people is… honestly, it's super weird at first. It's a little uncomfortable. You don't know what to do with your hands. "Do I act like a warthog…?" It was very strange at first, and I felt like we were working out the kinks of this a little bit as we were doing it. But it was nice to be able to interact with the other actors, because 90 percent of the time in animated productions, you're not with the other person.

Billy, what was it like working with Seth?

BE: Seth is so genuinely charming. His voice is so instantly recognizable, so unique, and there's so much charm and likability there, and a real vulnerability that I think fits Pumbaa perfectly. We're a really good mix: it's like a good yin and yang scenario with me and Seth. I've worked with him a little bit

SETH ROGEN
Selected Credits

FILMS
Long Shot, 2019
Fred Flarsky
The Disaster Artist, 2017
Sandy
Sausage Party, 2016
Frank, Sergeant Pepper
The Interview, 2014
Aaron Rapaport
Kung-Fu Panda 1, 2, 3, 2008–2016
Mantis
Pineapple Express, 2008
Dale Denton
Knocked Up, 2007
Ben Stone
The 40-Year-Old Virgin, 2005
Cal

TV
The League, 2011–2015
Dirty Randy
Undeclared, 2001–2003
Ron Garner
Freaks and Geeks, 1999–2000
Ken Miller

> ## "I'M A PRETTY BIG PERSON IN REAL LIFE, AND TIMON IS SMALL, BUT HE BEHAVES LIKE A BIG PERSON, AND HE HAS A BIG PERSONALITY."
> ### – BILLY EICHNER

before – I was in *Neighbors 2*, he's done *Billy on the Street* – but not like this.

When we both got the calls to do the movie, we exchanged some messages. His first message to me was just seven exclamation points. I knew exactly what he was referring to, how he felt, because it's incredible to be a part of it. It's mind-boggling that you get to be a part of something this big that has so much history to it and is so beloved.

How was it performing "Hakuna Matata"?

BE: Well, it's "Hakuna Matata." People really love [the song] and "Hakuna Matata" as a phrase has stayed with us since the original *The Lion King*. It's part of the cultural lexicon. On the one hand, we didn't want to mess with it too much, because it was pretty solid already, but at the same time, we've thrown in some jokes here and there. We didn't want to just copy what Nathan Lane and Ernie Sabella did with the original Timon and Pumbaa; we wanted to put our spin on it.

As much as we love and can't really surpass the original guys who did it, we are individuals, and so as with any role, you're bringing your individuality to it. Seth and I do have a funny, interesting chemistry, I think. Seth is not necessarily quiet, but there is a sweetness to him, and there's a sweetness to me too, but it's underneath a bit of showmanship. I think we're a good duo in that way.

What would you say Timon and Pumbaa's take on Simba is?

BE: It's pretty similar to the relationship in the original movie, which is Pumbaa really wants to keep him at first. Timon is a bit more hesitant, because Timon's really smart.

05

That's what I love about Timon: he's a little guy, but he's really smart. He's always three steps ahead of everyone else, maybe not physically – because he's smaller – but mentally. He knows that ultimately Simba's going to grow up to be a lion, and as little Timon, he's scared of that thought. But he falls in love with Simba the way that Pumbaa does, and they realize that they could maybe have a third friend. The whole time it's just him and Pumbaa wandering around trying to slam into vultures and filling up their days with that, so they're very excited about the fact that Simba could enter their family.

And that is what they create: a family. For a time they become Simba's surrogate parents, his friends, and his mentors. That's what "Hakuna Matata" is about; the great life lesson they give Simba is that for all the bad things that can happen to you, for all the tragic things that can happen to you, there can still be joy and fun. Don't sweat the small stuff, essentially.

Did you get to experience the virtual reality sets they created for the film?
BE: They put the goggles on my head, and they gave us a virtual tour of the land they were building, which was mind-boggling. I'm only a technology guy insofar as I need a phone that works well, so to say it's impressive is just this vast understatement. What they've done with this movie, the way they've put it together, it's really never been done before. Even since *The Jungle Book* the technology has evolved, so watching it all come together is mind-blowing.

What did you make of your characters when you saw the new versions of them?
BE: I think the spirit of the original Timon and Pumbaa is still alive – little Timon versus bigger Pumbaa; that relationship is still really funny to me and really sweet. For all the technology and the state-of-the-art animation that they've done, ultimately it really is about the characters and how they relate to each other, and the love between them, in addition to the comedy. So that's something that I really focused on.

Do you think this film will be a more intense experience than the original because it looks so real?
SR: Yeah, I think the stakes will probably feel higher than the original one, because there's a visceral sense of reality to it. You're more scared things are going to happen, because there's not that separation of it being a cartoon. They seem like real animals, and there's nothing that's scarier than the thought of animals getting hurt in a movie. People don't care if people get hurt in movies, but when animals are in peril, then it's really terrible.

Why do you think Disney has remade *The Lion King* – and *The Jungle Book* – in this way?
SR: They're good stories, and they seem to have picked talented

> **"I THINK THE STAKES WILL FEEL HIGHER THAN THE ORIGINAL FILM, BECAUSE THERE'S A VISCERAL SENSE OF REALITY TO IT."**
> **– SETH ROGEN**

people to make the movies as well. But also, for people who grew up with the original movies, it's exciting to see them told in a way that is as visually stimulating as the best things today. When they were made, at the time that animation was incredible. It's very beautiful and has a charm to it, but as far as something that's going to draw throngs of people to a theater, I think it needs to have a new and contemporary feeling.

They're great movies and stories, and they're picking incredibly interesting filmmakers for a lot of them; people that I myself am excited to work with, and I'm excited to see what they do with the projects.

There was certainly an emotional reaction from the crowd to the first announcement.
SR: It's a movie a lot of people grew up with, and they love it. I love it. I watched it so many times. It's one of those things where, in the best way – and I think that's why Jon is really ▶

04 Thanks to Timon and Pumbaa, Simba embraces a trouble-free philosophy (*Visual development artwork*)

05 The lush Cloud Forest becomes Simba's new home (*Visual development artwork*)

06 Timon's love for Simba outweighs his fear of the cub's natural predatory nature (*Visual development artwork*)

07

"FOR A LOT OF PEOPLE, *THE LION KING* IS THE FIRST TIME YOU SEE A REAL DEATH IN A MOVIE, AND IT'S THE FIRST TIME YOU SEE A REAL ROMANCE IN A MOVIE."
– SETH ROGEN

smart – you didn't know how much you wanted it until you saw it. Honestly, no one was sitting around thinking, "Man, it'd be cool if they made a version of *The Lion King* where the animals are real." But Jon did. Then when you see it, you're like, "Thank God they did that."

It's so gratifying and amazing. As someone who loves the original, the idea of getting to relive that story in a new way is really exciting. It's exciting knowing that I get to watch another version of that movie, and that it will deliver on all the stuff that I love and elevate it, because it is executed in such a new way. For a lot of people, *The Lion King* is the first time you see a real death in a movie, and it's the first time you see a real romance in a movie. There are a lot of first strong feelings cinematically that people have with the movie.

What has it been like to work with Jon Favreau?

BE: Jon's amazing. Sometimes you work with people and you don't know whether you can trust them, especially with comedy, because it's so subjective. But with Jon, I know his previous work, I know him as a person, and I fully and completely trust his point of view, so it's never really a fight. He's so collaborative. He chose me to be in it; I didn't have to audition for it – he knew my work, and he wanted me in this. So I trust the fact that he trusts me, and likewise. It's very much a two-way street.

He's been living with *The Lion King*, day-in, day-out for years, preparing this movie, so no one knows it better than he does. I brought whatever I brought to the table, and then I was very open to his feedback, and he was open to my bizarre ideas, and we met somewhere in between. But he's a joy, and he has so much passion for it.

He has cast a very diverse group, a very unique group. It's not just the biggest movie stars you could've possibly crammed into the movie; he really trusted his own instincts for who out there would bring something special to it, whether it's musically, comedically, or from an acting standpoint – or hopefully all three.

What experience will this film deliver for the audience?

BE: It's going to blow people's minds. If I'm being completely honest, I'm not even a guy who runs to see every single animated movie as soon as it comes out, and it really took my breath away. It's so beautiful. It's really emotional. It works on

08

07 Warthog Pumbaa is a gentle soul, despite his gruff exterior (*Visual development artwork*)

08 Timon – a little meerkat with big ideas (*Visual development artwork*)

09 The trio become firm friends for life (*Visual development artwork*)

> "SETH AND I DO KNOW EACH OTHER OFF CAMERA; WE ARE FRIENDS, WE'VE WORKED TOGETHER BEFORE, AND WE DO HAVE A FUNNY, INTERESTING CHEMISTRY."
> – BILLY EICHNER

many levels. I think it will honor what we already know and love about *The Lion King*, but put a unique, modern spin on it – and Jon's the perfect person to do it. He's really figured out that balance. People are going to be swept away. It's going to be very relatable and very emotional, but at the same time an escape to another place.

09

JON FAVREAU ON
THE
HYENAS

FLORENCE KASUMBA
KEEGAN-MICHAEL KEY
ERIC ANDRÉ

ith the hyenas, because of the photo-real nature of the film and the stakes feeling quite a bit higher and more real, having too much of a comedic take on the villains felt inconsistent with what we were doing. So we went for casting and performances and writing that felt a little bit more grounded in the stakes of the story, rather than the comedy that I think works very well in the '94 movie. Whoopi Goldberg [Shenzi in the original film], who I'm a huge fan of, did an amazing job, but as we tried to picture that characterization in this film, it always felt like a note that didn't fit. We wanted to raise the mystery and the stakes of the character of Shenzi, while offering some comic relief – because without it, it all felt wrong – [so we changed] the tone of the comedy.

"That's why we brought in Keegan-Michael Key and Eric André, who have improvisation and comedy backgrounds, but who are strong actors and story people as well. By having them together and exploring and improvising, we found how much, and to what extent, you could incorporate humor. Often it's seasoning to taste, depending on how the movie feels at any given time. So we have very broad performances, and very simple performances, and they work very well for both.

"For Shenzi, I remembered seeing Florence stand out even in the small role that she had in Marvel Studios' *Captain America: Civil War*. I felt that she had a really wonderful presence, and as I educated myself on her performances, she seemed really grounded and mysterious and cool. As Shenzi, she really brings a wonderful texture. Her voice has a wonderful texture, and she has incredible focus that you can see from her stage performances. I showed that to the animators and said, 'How do you make this character – this rendering that looks nothing like her – how do you bring that performance to it?' That was one of the challenges, but she gave us a wonderful foundation to build on."

01 The hyenas and Scar form a dastardly alliance (*Concept artwork*)
02 Shenzi and the hyenas are a foreboding presence in the Pride Lands (*Concept artwork*)

"WE WANTED
TO RAISE THE
MYSTERY AND
THE STAKES OF
SHENZI WHILE
OFFERING SOME
COMIC RELIEF."

**FLORENCE KASUMBA
& ERIC ANDRÉ**

SHENZI & AZIZI

As Shenzi, leader of the hyenas, Florence Kasumba found herself tapping into the malevolence of her character – a stark contrast to Eric André, who drew on his improv comedy background to craft the hyena Azizi. But both responded to the hyenas' newfound power, as well as to the timeless, primal nature of the material.

01 Scar and the hyenas – formidable partners in treachery (*Concept artwork*)

The Lion King – The Official Movie Special: **Florence, were you familiar with the original 1994 animated movie?**

Florence Kasumba: I remember it well. I actually have the DVD at home. When the movie came out, I was so excited to see it, and of course, I've watched it many times since then. Even my kids know it and all the songs. It's just a really beautiful movie.

Eric, were you a fan of the 1994 original?

Eric André: Oh yeah, I cried my eyes out. I was a mess. I was 11 when the 1994 version came out. It was a precious time for me. I was a very impressionable young boy.

What do you think makes the story of The Lion King so special?

FK: We have a strong connection to Simba, the cub, because of his father's death. We sympathize with him and ask ourselves what Simba's life will be like from now on. He creates a life for himself with unexpected friends, who help him grow up into a strong lion. He survives, conquers his fears and returns home to save Pride Rock. That's special.

EA: Isn't it based on Hamlet? The story is primal, and it's emotional. I think there are only six stories in human history, and they're repeated over and over again in different ways. This is a cool way of telling that story of Hamlet.

Eric, how did you get involved in this new version of The Lion King?

EA: I love Jon Favreau – I loved The Jungle Book from 2016 – and I love The Lion King. It was a pretty easy "Yes." I was stoked to do it. I love that we've done a 3D photo-realistic animated version of a classic, and the cast is amazing too.

Were you impressed by the technology?

EA: The tech is amazing. We saw little virtual reality mock-ups of each scene and how they animate to the VR shots that they come up with. It blows my mind. I have a really small little walnut brain, so I'm very easy to impress.

Did you do any research for your role?

EA: I actually did. I researched how hyenas and lions don't like each other at all, and they're constantly harassing each other.

What did you connect with in terms of fleshing out your character, Azizi?

EA: I loved the hyenas in the original, and I love that they're comedic relief for a pretty serious family movie. Also, I can laugh like the Cheshire Cat from Alice in Wonderland, so I'm pretty excited to play any character where I can laugh maniacally.

Florence, how does your character, Shenzi, fit into the story?

FK: Shenzi is a hyena, who wants power. She is a dominant member of her pack, and a threat – definitely someone you shouldn't trust. She doesn't feel comfortable with Scar, because he wants to betray "his pack." She sees him as a way to help the hyenas, even though hyenas and lions have always been at war. That is what makes working together with Scar so unusual. She knows he is dangerous, but trusts herself and her pack completely.

"SHENZI IS A DOMINANT MEMBER OF HER PACK – AND DEFINITELY SOMEONE YOU SHOULDN'T TRUST." – FLORENCE KASUMBA

02

Eric, how would you describe your character?

EA: Depending on what take they use, my character is kind of dumb and takes things very literally, and doesn't understand metaphors or figures of speech. Or, if they use the other, cattier take, my character is in a failed marriage – metaphorically, or maybe literally – with another hyena [named] Kamari. There's a lot of tension between the two. It's a bit of an odd couple dynamic.

What is the dynamic between Shenzi and the rest of the hyenas?

EA: Shenzi's the boss, and we don't really have any say in the decision-making. She's a dictator. We all live in fear of her.

FK: Shenzi is recognized as a leader and the brains of the hyenas. She feels responsible for them. When she enters, everybody's quiet. However, when it comes to a dangerous situation, they act as one.

How do the hyenas get involved in Simba's predicament?

FK: The first time Simba encounters the hyenas is because he doesn't listen to his father and goes past the border of the Pride

03

FLORENCE KASUMBA
Selected Credits

FILMS
Avengers: Infinity War,
2018
Ayo
Black Panther, 2018
Ayo
Wonder Woman, 2017
Senator Acantha
Captain America: Civil War, 2016
Security Chief
Transpapa, 2012
Tessi

TV
Deutschland 86, 2018
Rose Seithathi
Emerald City, 2017
East
Dominion, 2015
Daria
The Quest, 2014
Talmuh

02 The hyena pack looks on as fires rage in the Pride Lands (*Concept artwork*)

03 Scar enlists the support of the hyenas to ensure Mufasa is outnumbered (*Concept artwork*)

Lands. The hyenas find him and the only reason he doesn't get killed is because Mufasa shows up to save him. Scar sees an opportunity to use the hyenas for his purposes and forms an alliance with the hyenas. He needs them to kill Mufasa and Simba, so he can become king.

EA: Simba is coming of age, and he is challenging his father, indirectly – he's in a pre-adolescent rebellious phase. He goes into the Elephant Graveyard against his father's wishes. He goes to the wrong side of the tracks and more or less pays the price.

How does Scar convince the hyenas to side with him?
EA: Scar offers the head hyena a plan to get rid of Mufasa. Also, the way to a hyena's heart is through its stomach, so he offers them a lot of food. They're pretty simple creatures.

How do the hyenas react when Scar sells them out?
FK: They're not happy, when they find out. What do hyenas do when they are hungry? They eat; and when your food is directly in front of you – Scar – then you eat happily. Hyenas are grateful, when they don't have to hunt for their food. ▶

04 The hyenas cast a sinister shadow over the Pride Lands (*Concept artwork*)

05 The cunning Shenzi demands total respect from her pack (*Concept artwork*)

06 Simba is forced to run for his life after an encounter with the hyenas (*Concept artwork*)

07 Scar prepares to meet his fate (*Concept artwork*)

▶ **What can you tell us about your recording sessions, both alone and with the other cast members?**

FK: I had different experiences while recording. The first time, I worked with colleagues in a black box surrounded by cameras. That was fun, because we could also be physical and walk around. We could look at each other and try out different things. Another time, I was in a sound studio with a colleague. We didn't have the physical freedom, like in the black box, but we could still act with each other. I also worked alone in the sound studio. That was just like most recording experiences I've had, where you hear your cue and say your line. Then the director gives you notes and you try again.

What were the black box theater sessions like?

EA: I liked performing in the black box, because you had the freedom to move around. It was a very freeing and nurturing space, especially compared to regular animation voiceover, where you just stand in front of a microphone. It gave you the freedom to really get it in your body. It was nice to be more physical.

Does it help recording with another actor present?

FK: When I have a colleague in the studio, I can see their eyes, I can see their physical reaction, and I can react to that. It's nice to work with someone for those reasons, but I'm also trained to work alone. You could put a lamp in front of me

right now and then give me the voice from somewhere, and I could make that work too. You have to be flexible.

What was it like working with Keegan-Michael Key, who voices Kamari?

EA: Keegan's awesome. He's such a brilliant improviser, and has such a giant comedic brain. He makes life a lot easier. We didn't have time to meet before, but I felt so confident in his presence that I wasn't worried about it at all.

How did you find Jon Favreau as a director?

FK: He is incredibly professional and very clear on what he wants from you. He has a nice way to describe what he needs, and I appreciate that. He is also very funny. I remember being in the black box theater with him and laughing a lot. You forget that the room is full of people and can concentrate on the important things. I trust him and really liked working with him.

Did it make a difference to have a director who is also an actor?

FK: The nice thing is that he knows how it feels, when you are surrounded by a whole team in a studio, and have to stay focused and function under pressure. Because of his experience, he knows precisely how to help you in any moment.

EA: Jon's great, because he comes out of improv. He's a performer – he lives on both sides of the camera – so he's really easy to communicate with; just in his demeanor, he's such a

"THE TECH IS AMAZING. WE SAW LITTLE VIRTUAL REALITY MOCK-UPS OF EACH SCENE AND HOW THEY ANIMATE TO THE VR SHOTS THAT THEY COME UP WITH."
– ERIC ANDRÉ

ERIC ANDRÉ
Selected Credits

FILMS

Rough Night, 2017
Jake

Flock of Dudes, 2016
Mook

The Internship, 2013
Sid

TV

Disenchantment, 2018
Luci/Pendegrast

Man Seeking Woman,
2015–2017
Mike

Lucas Bros Moving Co,
2014–2015
Various

2 Broke Girls, 2013–2014
Deke

*Don't Trust the B**** in
Apartment 23,* 2012–2013
Mark Reynolds

The Eric André Show,
2012–present
Writer/host

07

Zen master. We talked a lot about what the game being played was – that's an improv term for the character's status.

What are you most excited for audiences to discover?

FK: The new technology is putting us as close to "real," as we've ever been in an animated film. Of course, there are all new voices and it will be exciting to hear them and find out how people react. Those who already loved Disney's *The Lion King* from 1994 will be in heaven, because everything will look new, yet familiar. Disney's *The Lion King* affected the entire world. Now, it is time for the next generation to experience this timeless story in a whole new way.

EA: *The Lion King* is a classic; the story is classic and has a lot of heart and emotion. I'm fortunate in that I get to be part of the comic relief of the movie… so I get to do my thing and act like a maniac. 🦁

JON FAVREAU ON
SARABI

ALFRE WOODARD

"We have Alfre Woodard playing Sarabi, which is one of the roles where we found there was room to add more, and help balance the cast. The original film was definitely weighted more toward the male roles; and certainly in the culture of a lion's pride, the female lions play a very important role. Also, there were, we felt, holes in the plot that we could smooth out involving Sarabi's character, even reconstituting versions of scenes that had existed and were cut from the '94 production, but also the original script and outtakes, as well as scenes that were included in the stage musical that weren't in the film.

"Having such a wonderful actor as Alfre Woodard – who brought gravitas to the role and the feeling of her being the queen and being Mufasa's counterpart – and cutting back to what was happening in the Pride Lands more than was done in the [original], provided us a really good counterbalance to what was happening in the Cloud Forest during that whole Hakuna Matata sequence. So she was wonderful. I'd never worked with her before, but she's great. So much of what she brings to her performance as an actor fortunately comes through in her voice, which is the hard part of casting films like this: the voice has to express as much or more than the actor does visually."

01

ALFRE WOODARD
Selected Credits

FILMS
Juanita, 2019
Juanita

Clemency, 2019
Bernadine Williams

Saint Judy, 2018
Judge Benton

Captain America: Civil War, 2016
Miriam

12 Years a Slave, 2013
Mistress Shaw

TV
Luke Cage, 2016-2018
Mariah Dillard

Empire, 2018
Renee

A Series of Unfortunate Events, 2017-2018
Aunt Josephine

True Blood, 2010-2012
Ruby Jean Reynolds

01 Sarabi is the matriarch of the Pride Lands' royal family (*Concept artwork*)
02 Strong and majestic, Sarabi is a revered queen (*Concept artwork*)

"THE ORIGINAL FILM WAS DEFINITELY WEIGHTED MORE TOWARD THE MALE ROLES; AND CERTAINLY IN THE CULTURE OF A LION'S PRIDE, THE FEMALE LIONS PLAY A VERY IMPORTANT ROLE".

JON FAVREAU ON
YOUNG
SIMBA

JD McCRARY

D, who's playing young Simba, is great. He is somebody that we found through the casting process, and it just so happens that in addition to being a bit of a YouTube sensation as a singer, he collaborated with Donald Glover on the last Childish Gambino album. When I told Donald that JD was going to be involved, he was very, very complimentary and excited.

"Having JD play the young Simba and hearing them both sing is wonderful. I think he not only brings tremendous humanity to the role, but so much personality in the way he sings. It's nice to get the opportunity to have actors who are both the performers and the singers. You get a certain amount of latitude when it comes to animated films to mix and match, and here, to have a kid that could belt it out and could also bring his personality to both the acting performance and the singing performance was great."

01

JD McCRARY
Selected Credits

FILMS
Little, 2019
Isaac

Atom: The Misadventures of a Real Super Hero, 2014
The Atom

TV
American Soul, 2019
Young Michael Jackson

The Paynes, 2018
Kenny Payne

I'm Dying Up Here, 2017
Adam's Bro Age 8

Teachers, 2017
Ayo

K.C. Undercover,
2015-2016
Young Ernie

02

"JD NOT ONLY BRINGS TREMENDOUS HUMANITY TO THE ROLE, BUT SO MUCH PERSONALITY IN THE WAY HE SINGS."

01 When Simba runs away from home, he finds a new family in Pumbaa and Timon (*Visual development artwork*)

02 Simba and Nala visit some winged neighbors during one of their many adventures (*Concept artwork*)

03 Simba is caught in a stampede and discovers that the Pride Lands can be a dangerous place (*Visual development artwork*)

01

JON FAVREAU ON
YOUNG NALA

SHAHADI WRIGHT JOSEPH

Shahadi actually played young Nala in a stage production of *The Lion King*, and I remembered seeing her in *Hairspray* live on TV. There was very little discussion about who should play young Nala – it was hers right from the beginning.

"It was great to have the kids around and seeing what the character was going to look like, then going into VR and exploring the environments and singing and performing. It was nice because it didn't disturb their lives too much as young kids. They came in, did their thing, and then they went and came back later to do another session. It wasn't the day-in, day-out grind it usually is for an actor, especially for kids, where it's hard. They have to do schooling and stuff. You saw them less often, but they came in with a lot of energy.

"Also, the wonder is they saw what we were doing with the footage. They're your first set of eyes that are watching it, and you get to see on their faces the excitement; both that they're in it, and also just as kids seeing this stuff come to life and seeing the magic. It was really fun for us, because it's a bit of a slow motion snail race, and everything's so secretive – it's not like you show it to a lot of people – so any moment where you get that feedback makes it exciting."

02

01 The Pride Lands are Nala and Simba's playground as cubs (*Concept artwork*)

02 Nala and Simba share a close bond from an early age (*Visual development artwork*)

03 Even the forbidding Elephant Graveyard doesn't dampen the young cubs' spirit of adventure (*Paintover*)

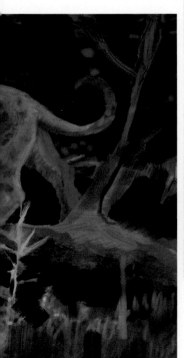

03

"THERE WAS VERY LITTLE DISCUSSION ABOUT WHO SHOULD PLAY YOUNG NALA – IT WAS SHAHADI'S RIGHT FROM THE BEGINNING."

JOHN OLIVER

ZAZU

For John Oliver, the prim and proper nature
of Zazu – hornbill advisor to King Mufasa –
was a character trait that he, as a Brit, could
very much relate to. In fact, the comedian
and TV host found all manner of parallels
with his British background to *The Lion King*
– some more apparent than others.

02

T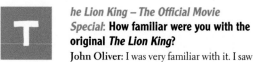*he Lion King – The Official Movie Special*: **How familiar were you with the original** *The Lion King*?

John Oliver: I was very familiar with it. I saw it when it came out, and then saw it again multiple times. Also, as a British person, we were all very excited that Elton John was doing songs for movies: "Our Elton, he's singing songs for Hollywood. See? We're still relevant!" That was basically the British take on it. "And look, Rowan [Atkinson] is in it as well! And Jeremy Irons! They still need us! Although usually as villains."

What was it about the original film that you connected with?

It's a really fun story. The songs were amazing; the animation was great; it felt like everything you'd want from a Disney movie. On top of that, our Elton wrote the songs. He won an Oscar®!

What drew you to this re-envisaged *The Lion King*?

I liked the idea of it. I watched the sequence of Simba opening his eyes. When you see what looks like a real lion

"AS A BRITISH PERSON, I RESPOND TO *THE LION KING* BECAUSE IT'S A STORY WHICH HAS A FUNDAMENTAL RESPECT FOR THE CONCEPT OF MONARCHY."

03

04

cub opening its eyes and see them glistening, any hesitancy you have over whether re-doing this is a good idea or not goes away pretty quickly. That first scene is absolutely mind-blowing – seeing the sunrise and seeing Simba have paint put on his forehead and being held up. It's absolutely incredible to witness it.

What makes this particular story so special?

Generationally, for people my age or that grew up with it, it's pretty much hardwired into your system as a classic, right from that opening scene.

As a British person, I respond to it because it's a story which has a fundamental respect for the concept of monarchy – there is a clear line of succession. If Zazu's doing anything as a bird, it's screaming defense of the monarchy – which logically, from the outside, makes no sense whatsoever and seems a very flawed way to govern any land. But you don't want to focus too much on a fundamentally broken system being grandfathered in, even when animals are involved. ▶

02 Zazu bears witness to Simba's momentous introduction at Pride Rock (*Concept artwork*)

03 Zazu is a loyal friend and mentor to both Mufasa and Simba (*Concept artwork*)

04 John Oliver on Zazu: "He is like a feathered GPS system." (*Paintover*)

▶ What can you tell us about your character?

Zazu is a bird who likes structure, who just wants things to be as they are. Again, I think there are British echoes there, because we tend to favor structure in lieu of having an emotional reaction to anything. You deflect all powerful feelings about anything into a process of how things should be done. That's Zazu in a nutshell.

How does Zazu fit into the story?

Zazu is there as a butler-esque figure, trying to provide service and structure to those who need it. Also, just by the fact he can fly, he's often telling people what is happening from a higher perspective – telling people that the person they're looking for is over there. He's like a feathered GPS system.

Can you personally relate to Zazu at all?

Can I relate to Zazu, the bird? I guess what you're asking is, have I ever felt like a hornbill? I mean, I've got a big nose – I'm beaky – so I relate to him in that sense. I can't fly. He can. That's a key difference between us.

How do I relate to Zazu the bird…? Well, I liked Zazu when I was a kid, so I'm a fan of him, and now I'm just [hoping] not to ruin him for future generations. I really loved the character because he was funny. I like funny characters in things, partly because they're not fully emotionally engaging in any situation. I like witty animals.

How would you describe the relationship between Simba and his family?

Complex. To put it extremely mildly, Simba has uncle issues. I guess it's a story about duty and responsibility.

What is Zazu's view of Mufasa and Simba?

Zazu is kind of in awe of Mufasa as a leader, and he takes it upon himself to take Simba under his physical and metaphorical wing to help him through the challenges in his young lion life. I think he feels a lot of responsibility for him – without being able to protect him in any physical way, due to the fact he's a bird, and everyone else can kill him.

How would you describe Scar?

Scar is your classic movie villain; again, British. He's clearly

> ## "ZAZU IS THERE AS A BUTLER-ESQUE FIGURE, TRYING TO PROVIDE SERVICE AND STRUCTURE TO THOSE WHO NEED IT."

05 Zazu gives Mufasa an update during his daily morning patrol (*Concept artwork*)

a Machiavellian character – he's not a pleasant lion. I can remember him scaring the life out of me as a child. When did the original *The Lion King* come out? 1994? I was 17. [*Laughs*] I think in my head I've kind of justified being scared of it because I was six. I was actually 17 when it came out. There's no way to make that answer less humiliating. I was very frightened as a 17-year-old by the animated lion that is Scar. It is frightening though, right? That Elephant Graveyard… I was very frightened.

How did you find the recording sessions?

It was really fun messing around with the script and interacting with the other characters. It wasn't my first time doing animation, but it was the first time doing it in this particular way of changing up little scenes or adding stuff in. It was fun going back and forth, changing lines and throwing in extra little bits, especially knowing they would animate off whatever weird extra rhythms we did.

I've always loved doing animation because it's such a fun

JOHN OLIVER
Selected Credits

FILMS
Wonder Park, 2019
Steve
The Smurfs 2, 2013
Vanity Smurf
The Smurfs, 2011
Vanity Smurf

TV
Last Week Tonight with John Oliver, 2014-present
Himself
The Late Show with Stephen Colbert, 2018
Paul McCartney
Danger Mouse, 2016–2017
Augustus P. Crumhorn IV
The Simpsons, 2014
Booth Wilkes-John
Community, 2009-2014
Professor Ian Duncan/
Xim-Xam/Mix-Max
Robot Chicken, 2014
Serpentor/British Gentleman
Rick and Morty, 2013
Dr. Xenon Bloom
The Daily Show, 2012
Correspondent

"IT WAS FUN GOING BACK AND FORTH, CHANGING LINES AND THROWING IN EXTRA LITTLE BITS, ESPECIALLY KNOWING THEY WOULD ANIMATE OFF WHATEVER WEIRD EXTRA LINES WE DID."

break from what I regularly do, which is stare at the state of the world and try not to quietly die inside. So it was nice to do *The Lion King*, because it was the exact opposite of my regular day.

How was working with Jon Favreau?

It was a blast. He has a clear sense in his head of what he needs, and then he's very good at leaving some stuff loose, which hopefully will mean that the way the characters interact with the animation doesn't feel quite so rigid, so it

doesn't sound as scripted as it actually is. Just keeping in little stumbles, or odd rhythms of reads, or characters interrupting each other, means that it feels a little bit more alive.

What experience will audiences have watching this movie?

It's pretty magical [and] pretty overwhelming when you see that first scene. The thing I liked about *The Lion King* the first time was the scale of it; the scale of the animation felt new. This is going to feel the same way again, because unless you work in this particular world of animation, it's barely fathomable to know how it is physically possible to do the things they have done here. It's very hard to rationalize. Your head gets confused over the fact you are not actually looking at actor animals. It's incomprehensible how much work has gone into every single frame of what they've done.

The Lion King is one of the most heartfelt and personal stories to most people, so it's a huge responsibility that they've taken on.

Rafiki – the wise
shaman of the
Pride Lands – is
portrayed vocally
by John Kani (*Black
Panther, Captain
America: Civil War,
Coriolanus*)
(*Concept artwork*)

JAMES CHINLUND
PRODUCTION DESIGNER

PRODUCTION DESIGN

With its virtual reality sets, the new reimagining of *The Lion King* has revolutionized filmmaking. The production team have also gone above and beyond in their search for a real-world basis for those VR environments. Production Designer James Chinlund explains the process of location scouting in both the real and virtual worlds.

01 The film's wildlife is inspired by the animals found in Kenya's Maasai Mara National Reserve (*Visual development artwork*)

"BEING ABLE TO CONTROL THE WORLD TO THE DEGREE YOU CAN IN A MOVIE LIKE THIS IS AN AMAZING OPPORTUNITY."

he Lion King – The Official Movie Special: How does it feel to be involved with such a pioneering production?

James Chinlund: This opportunity has been a really exciting one. When I saw *The Jungle Book*, as a traditional, live-action production designer I suddenly got the sweats. I could see how quickly the technology was advancing and was worried about being left behind. So when the opportunity came to work in this new way, I was so excited about the chance. Being able to control the world to the degree you can in a movie like this is an amazing opportunity.

There are big differences in the workflows but also some real similarities. We scouted in Africa, looking for locations that would inspire our sets, then came back to the studio and built sets that would support the narrative. So it was different, but at the same time felt very familiar to me.

Did Jon Favreau give you a mandate when you visited Africa?

Jon was really invested in delivering a true representation of Africa, and making sure that we delivered it in the highest resolution possible. So the mandate for me from Jon was to get out there, find the elements we needed to create the world of *The Lion King*, and see what parts of this world would work for the story.

Where did you go, and what did you experience?

I capped off 11 days of the most incredible high-speed scouting I've ever done in my life at the bottom of a ravine on Mount Kenya. When we were at the Maasai Mara, I saw the most beautiful collection of wildlife and animals. The density there is unparalleled in the world; to be able to see cheetahs, lions,

JAMES CHINLUND
Selected Credits

FILMS:
War for the Planet of the Apes, 2017
Dawn of the Planet of the Apes, 2014
The Avengers, 2012
Towelhead, 2007
The Fountain, 2006
The Final Cut, 2004
25th Hour, 2002
Auto Focus, 2002
Storytelling, 2001
Lift, 2001
Requiem for a Dream, 2000
Speed of Life, 1999

02 The lush Cloud Forest location was inspired by Mount Kenya (*Visual development artwork*)

03 Pelicans enjoy a misty dawn (*Visual development artwork*)

04 Some of Timon's fellow meerkats who inhabit the Pride Lands (*Visual development artwork*)

"THE MANDATE WAS TO FIND THE ELEMENTS WE NEEDED TO CREATE THE WORLD OF *THE LION KING*, AND SEE WHAT PARTS OF THIS WORLD WOULD WORK FOR THE STORY."

elephants, and hyenas – all the characters in our movie – up close and in such an intimate setting, was so exciting for me.

What was your process in the real-world location-scouting phase of the film?

Everywhere we went, we tried to get an aerial look to get a lay of the land. We certainly had targets that were generated from our research in L.A., but working with the local guides and our chopper pilots was an amazing resource for us in terms of ▶

05

▶ digging in and really combing out the best of Kenya in such a short amount of time. In 11 days we really saw most of the country and the treasures it has to offer.

What were the high points for you?

Getting to see lions up close was a new thing for me, and spending so much time close to the big cats really gave me a new sense of respect for them and the way they live. That was certainly a highlight.

I think all the work we did circling around Mount Kenya

and exploring that world – such a magical place, with so many different microclimates and mystical, wild forests – was really unexpected and exciting. It was an incredible location full of treasure for us. Exploring the grasslands and getting a true sense of the world – the rules of the landscape – up close was really exciting.

Is it true that you found Young Simba on this trip?

On our last day in the Mara, I went out on a scout with Andy, the Animation Supervisor, and our guide. We came across a

05 Father and son enjoy a majestic sunrise over their kingdom (*Visual development artwork*)

pride of lionesses and their cubs. They had just feasted on an eland, so it was fresh action from the night before, and quite a scene – they were all super stuffed and sleepy. During that time when we were watching them, a young cub woke up from his morning nap, and we got to see him move through the pride. Watching his interactions with each of the lionesses – greeting each other – and then wandering over to the eland to have some more breakfast, right away you had a sense that this guy was special. It was so exciting for us to see him so close – it was a real find. ▶

"GETTING TO SEE LIONS UP CLOSE WAS A NEW THING FOR ME, AND SPENDING SO MUCH TIME CLOSE TO THE BIG CATS REALLY GAVE ME A NEW SENSE OF RESPECT FOR THEM AND THE WAY THEY LIVE."

"I CAME BACK TO L.A. WITH A MASSIVE LIBRARY OF MEMORIES AND EXPERIENCES."

06

06 Thanks to their research, Chinlund and his team were able to recreate the Kenyan scenery with photo-real accuracy in the new *The Lion King* film (*Visual development artwork*)

07 & 08 The Maasai Mara National Reserve provided endless inspiration for the wildlife depicted in the reimagined *The Lion King* (*Visual development artwork*)

▶ Can you tell us a little about the crew you took with you to capture those moments?

Our chopper pilot knew the country like the back of his hand, and he got us deep into the forest and out into the grasslands with incredible precision. I was often with Adam Valdez [VFX Supervisor] and Audrey Ferrara [Environment Supervisor], both from MPC [Moving Picture Company], and we had a digital cataloguer with us named Ben, who basically helped us capture all the textures and shapes. We did some photogrammetry of big rock formations and things. We went back to L.A. with a full library of assets; the richest research library I could possibly have imagined. It was an amazing time.

What did you personally take away from the trip?

I would say it was one of the greatest gifts I've had as a production designer, to be able to spend that much time on the ground in such a beautiful place. With all the tools, and being able to fly around and touch down everywhere we wanted to see, it was an unbelievable scout. I came back to L.A. with a massive library of memories and experiences. 🦁

07

VR FILMMAKING

James Chinlund describes the process of using virtual reality to create the world of the new *The Lion King* film...

"We start with an absolutely empty space – a digital void. Literally, we're designing the world from the ground up. As we start to unpack these various spaces, our process in the art department is to build the world first, and then find the space within the world that would be appropriate to the set.

"For example, we scouted a space known as the Cloud Forest, which is the site of 'Hakuna Matata' and all those classic sets, so we knew more or less that it was a mountain valley, and it needed to have a river in it and a waterfall. Reaching back to the research from our scout in Kenya, we were exploring the areas around Mount Kenya that had features relevant to the Cloud Forest.

"We used photogrammetry of Mount Kenya itself. MPC went and photographed the mountain extensively, so we actually had a digital model of the mountain. Then, in a traditional set design way, we sculpted a river valley, and then we put all that into the computer. I was able to go into the virtual space myself and scout that preliminary model. Within that preliminary model we found various spaces that would be appropriate for the different sequences, like 'Can You Feel the Love Tonight.' We knew we needed a waterfall, so we designed that into the space, but then we were able to go in there and say, 'I wish it was deeper.'

"Building a world has been an amazing process. Much like a video game, it's an open world: you can fly anywhere and then identify the various spaces within it that you want to shoot in.

"Coming into the project I really didn't know what to expect, but other than the slight VR nausea, it's really similar to a real-world location scout. Guys are moving around the space, going up to check out different angles and offering possibilities. It's so exciting that we could build the world to a high enough resolution, and with enough interconnectivity between the spaces, that they really have the opportunity to fly around freely and use the camera to see alternate angles.

"I do feel it's going to be interesting when I go back to traditional live action, to see how we might use this technology in those situations – where we might actually want to build a proxy of the world to be able to scout and check out angles that you wouldn't necessarily have access to, for example. Building the world of *The Lion King* has been a moment of powerful synergy, bringing together so many disparate technologies to build a new world."

08

ANDREW R. JONES
ANIMATION SUPERVISOR

ANIMATION

One of the big challenges of *The Lion King* for Animation Supervisor Andrew R. Jones was to strike a balance between the naturalness and believability of the film's animal stars, and their performances as characters. Achieving that entailed the utilization of the movie's revolutionary virtual reality stage.

01 In the Cloud Forest, Simba regards Nala as they drink from a stream (*Rendered film frame*)

ANDREW R. JONES
Selected Credits

FILM
The Jungle Book, 2016
World War Z, 2013
Avatar, 2009
The Lovely Bones, 2009
Superman Returns, 2006
I, Robot, 2004
Final Fantasy: The Spirits Within, 2001
Godzilla, 1998
Titanic, 1997

02 Zazu attempts to keep a boisterous young Simba on the straight and narrow (*Rendered film frame*)

03 Simba as a cub, alert and full of detail, character, and color (*CG render*)

04 Young Nala, beautifully rendered by the animators (*CG render*)

The Lion King – The Official Movie Special: **What was your initial reaction when this new iteration of *The Lion King* was proposed to you?**

Andrew R. Jones: When Jon Favreau called me and said he was going to do it, my first feeling was excitement, because as an animator, this was the Holy Grail for me. It was one of the most beautiful animated films ever, and still is. It's one of the most powerful stories, and it had a big effect on me when I saw it. Now, to be able to work on it as an animation supervisor has been a dream come true.

To me, it seemed logical to take what we did with *The Jungle Book* and move it another step forward, with all the computer-generated environments that look completely real, computer-generated characters that feel and look completely real, but they're giving the exact performance that Jon wants. It sounded like a lot of fun. When I'm challenged, that's when I have the most fun, and bringing these characters to life in a very believable, realistic way – making people scratch their heads and wonder what they're looking at – is the most fun of all.

What was behind the decision to use a virtual reality stage on this movie?

The VR stage adds an element of live action. It creates the feeling that we're finding it in the frame, we're finding these moments that are spontaneous and interesting, the way a cinematographer like Caleb Deschanel finds interesting aspects of what the characters are doing. That's something that if you go the other route, where you go from storyboards to layout to animation, it's all predefined shots, and somehow less spontaneous, less live action.

"BRINGING THESE CHARACTERS TO LIFE IN A VERY BELIEVABLE, REALISTIC WAY – MAKING PEOPLE SCRATCH THEIR HEADS AND WONDER WHAT THEY'RE LOOKING AT – IS THE MOST FUN OF ALL."

02

03

04

So in a sense you're honoring classical, practical filmmaking?

I think we are. We're honoring any human errors in terms of camera work. That's where it goes wrong a little in a fully animated feature, where the cameras can feel perfect, and everything's perfectly framed and perfectly timed, and it gives it that aspect of feeling very honed. This feels like found footage, a bit more documentary style, because you're not anticipating everything the characters are going to do or could possibly do, and the camera makes you feel that way.

Take us through the animation process on this film.

The process is, we get animation approved on a very rudimentary scale, then it goes to the VR stage, and they shoot all sorts of coverage on that animation – wide shots, dolly shots, whatever Caleb can dream up. Then it goes to editorial. They cut it together like live-action footage, and then from there we get to turn over a sequence that goes to MPC [Moving Picture Company]. These are basically the shots that Jon is happy with in the sequence.

> "THESE CHARACTERS ALL HAVE TO PERFORM LIKE EVERYBODY IMAGINES THEY WOULD, BUT AT THE SAME TIME WE'RE REFERENCING A CARTOON VERSUS SOMETHING VERY REALISTIC."

From there, it goes back into the animation pipe, where from a pre-viz animation we go into final animation. We get into all the details of performance and nitpicking things, and there might be slight changes, especially with physics and the way these animals move, or when they tackle each other, like the cubs. You really get into the details of the weight and the timings and how that's going to look. That might inspire a ▶

05

separate camera move, so at that point, they may go back to the VR stage to be reshot as a long take with more refined animation, so that the camera can be more indicative of what's happening. Then we render it; the environments are all painstakingly done – and actually extremely beautiful – and hopefully it all comes together.

Is it a balancing act between achieving the photo-real look, and getting the desired level of performance from the characters?

It's exactly treading that line. These characters all have to perform like everybody imagines they would, but at the same time we're referencing a cartoon versus something very realistic. There's a lot of anthropomorphic emotion in the cartoon, a lot of human expression and movement that we can't do. So we've got to find a cleverer way to do it with realistic animals in terms of how we animate them and how we move them. It all has to feel natural to their ability, yet get across the emotion that we're trying to get for that scene.

Why not use motion or facial capture?

Jon's very sensitive to that – the good things about motion capture, and the bad things. Motion capture is really good at capturing details and emotion, as long as you're going one to one. If you're going from an actor that looks like that character and is maybe wearing some digital makeup, like we did in *Avatar*, that works. But when you're going to a cat, a completely different physicality than a human, it doesn't relate.

You have to find an animator's eye to translate those performances in a way that's believable with what a cat's morphology can do, but try to get the same kind of emotion out of a very realistic cat motion. Even just taking lip-sync, we go very, very subtle. We keep it more like the anatomy of what the jaw can really do, but still try to get a believability that these characters are speaking.

Is it easier or harder to create believable digital animal characters than human ones?

To me, it's right in between the step of having digital humans, where the bar is at the very highest. We're so used to seeing humans – we talk to them every day – that we notice even the smallest inconsistencies. With big cats, we are aware of them, but there might not be as great a degree of difficulty in terms of nailing it exactly. So I think we have a little bit of leeway. But at the same time, everybody is very familiar with seeing *Big Cat Diary* and other shows – we've seen tons of footage on them. So everything has to be right to pull this off.

> ## "IT ALL HAS TO FEEL NATURAL TO THE ANIMAL'S ABILITY, YET GET ACROSS THE EMOTION THAT WE'RE TRYING TO GET FOR THAT SCENE."

We also have an amazing team in London that's good at getting all the details right – getting the fur right, and the muscle and the skin simulation and all the stuff that's very, very difficult to get right. Getting that level of detail and being able to really pull it off is the magic trick that we're trying to do.

Is this movie as cutting edge as it gets?

We're taking everything we learned on *The Jungle Book* and pushing it another few levels up. We're taking a lot of the stuff we learned about skin movement, and muscle movement, and how the characters take the weight and how believable that is, and pushing it to that next level. With me, it's also the render quality of these characters, but we're stepping up on that as well – the way the fur takes light in very realistic manners.

What really helps sell these things is getting that documentary feel of longer lenses and shallow depth of field – the sense that you're photographing this animal in its own environment. It feels like these environments are vast, that you're out on the plains of Africa and watching this story unfold. That's something Jon is really keen to do: make the story feel very big and broad, but then draw you into these characters.

06

"WE'RE TAKING EVERYTHING WE LEARNED ON *THE JUNGLE BOOK* AND PUSHING IT ANOTHER FEW LEVELS UP."

05 Poised and elegant, Sarabi watches over her young cub (*Rendered film frame*)

06 A close-up of Sarabi, showcasing the incredible detail of the rendering (*Rendered film frame*)

Where does this desire to reach the next level come from?

It comes from our captain, from Jon. He's meticulous with the details. If anything's slightly off, if it's not quite right – even a fly that goes by camera – he'll pick it up. He's really good with physics; he's good with light and quality of image; he's got a very good eye; and he's tough to please, especially when it comes to realism and physics and trying to get all the details right.

Would you categorize this film as live action, or would you say it's animation?

I think we're trying to be live action, but the performances are animated. We're trying to disguise that as much as possible. We're trying to feel like we just found the exact right moment for these performances. Obviously we have lip-sync, but it's really a study of real animals, a study of how they move and behave, and how we can fit that into these behaviors that we need them to be in, or these emotions that we need them to be in. It is animated by the animators – there are about a hundred animators working on it – but in the end they're supposed to be invisible, like all visual effects films that I work on. The effects are supposed to be invisible.

07

07 Mufasa is king
of all he surveys
(*CG render*)

08 Mufasa's
musculature can be
seen in detail
(*CG render*)

09 Mufasa, King
of Pride Rock
(*CG render*)

▶ **The film does feel very grounded.**

That's very true. That's why Jon hired someone like Caleb, a very traditional director of photography, to try to come up with traditional camera work that makes it feel grounded, that will make it feel less CG, less like big fly-by camera work that can only have been done in the computer.

With the live action feel of the film, did you have to be conscious of it becoming too scary?

It's something Jon was super aware of. When I showed him the scene of Mufasa's death in animation, he got choked up. He was tearing up and it wasn't even rendered! He said, "When this is real, this is going to be very heavy and very strong and powerful." He started grappling with how we could curb it a little, because it was too intense.

The answer lies in how you frame it, how you compose it, what choices you make in terms of going a little wider so we're not so intense, and not clearly seeing the father. Certain choices that they made in the original film, where Simba is trying to wake his dad up and pushing on him, we knew we couldn't do that, so we've done a subtle moment where possibly he touches and possibly he doesn't. Because it's more

"WHAT REALLY HELPS SELL THESE THINGS IS GETTING THAT DOCUMENTARY FEEL OF LONGER LENSES AND SHALLOW DEPTH OF FIELD – THE SENSE THAT YOU'RE PHOTOGRAPHING THIS ANIMAL IN ITS OWN ENVIRONMENT."

realistic, those moments become almost more gruesome and have more weight. You don't have the drawn frame to say this is just a cartoon still. It's very tricky.

With comedy, Jon's always good at finding that, and finds it more in the characters' charm. Timon and Pumbaa are a lot of fun, and the way that Billy Eichner and Seth Rogen play them, there are a lot of charming little moments between the two of them that sit well with the way the characters are designed. I think we're going to find some laughter through charm and through the cuteness of the characters, and how they're performing. That goes a long way.

CALEB DESCHANEL
DIRECTOR OF PHOTOGRAPHY
CINEMATOGRAPHY

For Caleb Deschanel – a cinematographer with an impressive pedigree in filmmaking – *The Lion King* represented something of a leap into the unknown. Or so he believed: in fact, many of the techniques and methods Deschanel had spent 40 years perfecting were replicated in the film's cutting-edge virtual reality space.

01 Simba shows a newly arrived Nala around the Cloud Forest *(Concept artwork)*

The Lion King – The Official Movie Special: As a cinematographer you're used to working in a more traditional manner. How did Jon Favreau convince you to come on board this very technologically advanced new take on *The Lion King*?

Caleb Deschanel: I wasn't sure about it at first. I was worried it would be like revisiting calculus class – all math and technology. I loved the story and was excited to work with Jon. But it took a while to warm up to the idea of making a film this way – in virtual reality. But the tools [Visual Effects Supervisor] Rob Legato and Magnopus developed mimicked the tools I was used to using when filming live action. I got excited about that.

Early on, before we started shooting, I went with Rob to Magnopus' offices downtown and we played around with the equipment they were developing and even filmed a shot that is used in the movie. This really sold me. Once we started I was surprised how deeply immersed you could become in this kind of environment and filmmaking and how inventive you could be.

How does filming in virtual reality differ from live-action filmmaking?

Honestly it's not much different from filming on a movie set that is designed and built for a movie – except there is nothing physical there. You put on goggles and see the location and the animals in 3D space; you can move around it from any angle, you can walk through it, or fly over it with the tools they give you. You just can't touch it or sit on it.

In a weird way, what we filmed was reduced to the pure visual world that is the essence of a movie. When you prepare for any movie you read a script, the director casts the movie, you find locations or build sets, the actors perform, and you shoot it. In the end, the movie is reduced to what you project on a screen – what you took the time to film no longer exists. The actors go on to other movies as other characters, the sets are torn down, the locations go back to whatever they were before you got there, and all you are left with is a ribbon of film that has recorded all that went on in front of the camera. The process we used just skips the necessity of physical sets or real locations and live actors. It is a computer rendering of the essence of filmmaking.

Did you have any concerns about the process?

One of the worries that concerned me from the beginning had to do with performance. I love working with actors and watching them create a character. Studying the actors and understanding their performances always inspires me when filming. The way

"WHEN I SAW WHAT JON HAD DONE WITH *THE JUNGLE BOOK*, I WAS SO IMPRESSED AND AMAZED – IT WAS SUCH EXTRAORDINARY WORK, AND NOW *THE LION KING* WAS GOING TO BE THE NEXT GENERATION."

02

CALEB DESCHANEL
Selected Credits

FILM
Never Look Away, 2018
Jack Reacher, 2012
Killer Joe, 2011
My Sister's Keeper, 2009
The Spiderwick Chronicles, 2008
The Passion of the Christ, 2004
National Treasure, 2004
The Hunted, 2003
The Patriot, 2000
Message in a Bottle, 1999
The Natural, 1984
The Right Stuff, 1983
Being There, 1979

you film an actor affects the emotions that come across. So I was worried the animation of the characters would be too limited or too crude to make those kind of judgments. In the early stages of filming the animation was limited – but as we went along it got better and better to the point that I could sense the feelings and emotions of all the characters. It was a big relief.

An important aspect of the prep for the filming was shooting video of a number of the actors as they were recording their voices – we watched and could study their performances. The animators used the performances to inspire the animation. But know that the genius of the animation is that it expresses all this character and emotion without betraying the actual real-life behavior of all these animals. Pretty amazing.

I always loved the story, and I've always loved to make children's movies – ever since my kids were little. I loved to take my kids to movies and see their excitement and wonder at

what they were seeing. Now this is a movie I can see with my grandkids – it seemed like a perfect project. When I saw what Jon had done with *The Jungle Book*, I was so impressed and amazed – it was such extraordinary work, and now *The Lion King* was going to be the next generation. I just sensed that it would be incredibly exciting if I could get past my worry about working with all this incredible technology. But Jon kept his eye on telling the story – using the technology at his disposal – but never losing track of the characters and the adventure he was creating. The movie is so different from anything I'd ever done and I always like to do projects that are unlike other films I have worked on.

Was it a surprise to be doing what is in essence live-action filmmaking but in a virtual reality space?

What's incredible is that it was not all that different from filming a live-action film. All the tools were designed to make it as close to making a live-action movie as possible. We had dollies and dolly track. At first we thought that making a movie utilizing VR, anyone could move the dolly, but we soon discovered we needed a real experienced dolly grip to push the dolly. It's a real art. So we hired a dolly grip. We started out having the computer follow focus – but it never felt right. So we brought in my regular first assistant cameraman to follow focus; there is an art to that as well. We had gear heads with wheels and fluid heads for following the action. We had cranes and eventually used a Steadicam. It's pretty amazing how many tools we had that were made to mimic what I am used to. And along the way we kept inventing new ways and new tools to make filming more versatile and more exciting. We could repurpose any of the pieces of equipment to do something different than what it was designed for. ▶

02 Nala and Simba share a drink in the Cloud Forest (*Rendered film frame*)

We had to constantly remind ourselves to adhere to certain rules of reality filmmaking – to not let it get out of hand – to use our instincts and experience to judge what would make the audience feel it was real. We could literally do anything – but that "anything" could destroy the experience if we went too far.

We had an incredible research department, and we studied a lot of films, and photos and paintings to try to get to the spirit of what this world should look and feel like. You study some of the great movies of all time with incredible visual storytelling, like *Lawrence of Arabia* or *Spartacus*, and you realize that as they were filming, the sun would move, and the light would change position in each shot, but the scenes would cut together seamlessly. We realized that if you make everything perfect, it doesn't actually feel real anymore. The tendency in CGI is to set the lighting and leave it in one place for all the shots in a sequence. But that is not what happens in the real world. The sun moves all day long. We ended up moving the sun in almost every shot to create the film reality we wanted.

To get to the feel of the movie, we'd reverse engineer the whole process of making movies. You'd think about how you ended up with certain scenes in the live-action movies you've done. Then we let that be our guide for making this movie. I was watching a film I worked on, *The Patriot*, and I realized

04

03 Simba follows Pumbaa and Timon through the Cloud Forest, echoing the classic movie (*Rendered film frame*)

04 Simba and Nala enjoy the tranquility of the Cloud Forest (*Concept artwork*)

"WHAT'S INCREDIBLE IS THAT IT WAS NOT ALL THAT DIFFERENT FROM FILMING A LIVE-ACTION FILM. ALL THE TOOLS WERE DESIGNED TO MAKE IT AS CLOSE TO MAKING A LIVE-ACTION MOVIE AS POSSIBLE."

there are so many shots in the movie that were inspired by a particular moment in time as we were filming – the nature of the sunlight that day, the way the shadows of the clouds were moving across the fields, the way the sun disappeared behind a cloud. We didn't have that in VR, so we had to create our own inspiration, and that was an extra element to guide the shooting.

So did you create your own boundaries as to what you could and couldn't do in the VR space?

Yes. You definitely create boundaries and limitations to adhere to – to create our sense of what is real, but we'd constantly reassess those boundaries as well. In traditional documentaries with wild animals they'd use long lenses off in the distance because of safety or other practicalities. But if we did this it would severely limit our understanding of the characters and telling of the story. And yet we wanted the feeling of what is possible in real life. The incredible ingenuity of modern documentaries about animals – like *Planet Earth II* and some other films using remote cameras and infrared film, etc. – inspired us to be more free.

When we were in Africa, the animals came uncomfortably close at times, and this was a revelation. The animals would get used to us driving around in a Rover or pickup truck and would ignore us and go about their business. When you're looking through the camera, you lose track of where you are at times – the danger is lost on you. At one point I was following a lion walking closer and closer. The shot went out of focus and I was about to chastise my AC, Tommy, for missing the focus. It turned out the lion was inside the 12-foot minimum distance for the lens. When I looked up from the eyepiece I saw Kenny, our key grip – sitting on the tail gate – wiping his brow in mock relief. The lion had come to within a few feet of him.

The truth is we just came to an understanding with these wild animals. We could film them up close and see their reactions and expressions and they would not attack us.

We filmed lots of footage in Africa and used it as reference, and we had wonderful research of other material for everything we were going to be filming. We had to make ourselves believe what we were doing. We were the first audience for the movie.

When we were shooting, I would sometimes miss a shot – a lion would go out of frame a bit, or I'd misframe, so we'd go back and shoot it again, trying to make it perfect. But when we'd compare the takes, sometimes the "mistake" was actually better, because it felt more organic to the process of making a movie. You'd have a feeling of some humanity guiding the filming. It was not mechanical and perfect. You'd have a sense of the actions, the scenes, being observed – that there was a human point of view. I think it gives the film a certain ▶

05

06

► character that added to the sense of reality created by the incredible animation.

You mentioned creating your own inspiration; how does that work in practice?

We're talking about a world in which we're missing the surprises and accidents that often influence a movie and make it better than you imagined. Every time you replayed a scene, in our world it was the same as the time before. The performance was set. So we tried to create an imperfect world in which little accidents could happen.

We got there with repetition. We could have a thousand wildebeests return to their starting position in a second, so it gave us the time and opportunity to try lots of new ideas and discover something special in the way we filmed it. This became our serendipity. If you knew you only had one chance at filming

> **"WE COULD HAVE A THOUSAND WILDEBEESTS RETURN TO THEIR STARTING POSITION IN A SECOND, SO IT GAVE US THE TIME AND OPPORTUNITY TO TRY LOTS OF NEW IDEAS."**

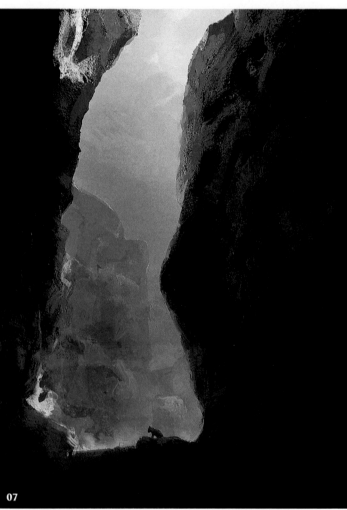

07

the hundreds of wildebeests charging through a canyon, you'd set up a number of cameras and shoot the most tried and true shots – from well thought out positions you are sure will record all the important action. You would not waste time on some "crazy" ideas that had a low percentage of success. But we had the freedom to try those crazy ideas – because we didn't have to wait an hour for the wranglers to drive the wildebeests back to the start. And sometimes these crazy angles or camera moves turned out to be surprising and perfect for the movie.

I was talking about doing a lot of research: we'd look at these great movies and see that there's a lot of failure in them. There's lots of failure in everything we do. But in the end you get to what you need to tell the story. When you're trying to achieve something you dream, it often cannot be created the way you imagined. There is so much trial and error and in the end it is our instincts that guide us. You accept certain

flaws because they make you believe. I like to think that there is a reality that we experience every day – and there is the emotional reality of a story we are telling. If we can guide the audience to this emotional reality, they will believe what they aspire to believe from the story we are telling. If they stepped back, it might not seem real at all – but if we take them to that place in the story, then they will believe. That is what we try to do when we make a movie.

How would you summarize your experience on this film?
If somebody had told me five years ago that I'd be working on a movie at the cutting edge of film technology, I would have thought they were crazy. But it's actually much more fun than I thought it would be. I find myself using my instincts in the same way, and with the same eye towards telling a story. But with a vast amount of additional freedom to dream and imagine. 🦁

05 The fateful wildebeest stampede in the canyon (*Concept artwork*)

06 The face of Mufasa is visible in the clouds, as lightning strikes around Simba (*Concept artwork*)

07 A heartbreaking moment, as Simba finds the body of his father (*Concept artwork*)

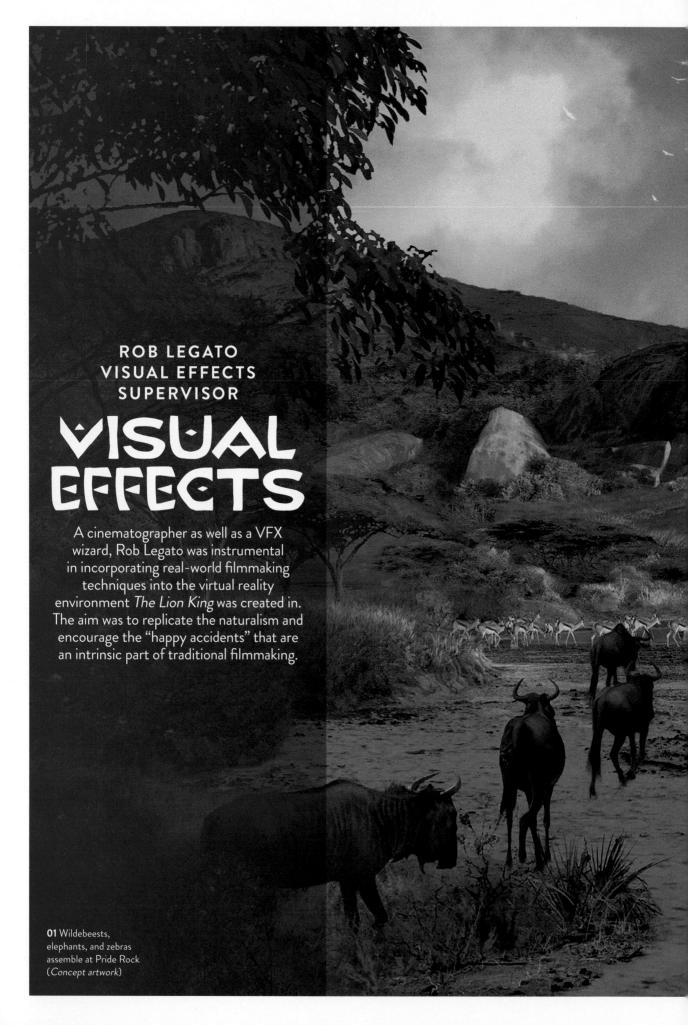

ROB LEGATO
VISUAL EFFECTS
SUPERVISOR

VISUAL EFFECTS

A cinematographer as well as a VFX wizard, Rob Legato was instrumental in incorporating real-world filmmaking techniques into the virtual reality environment *The Lion King* was created in. The aim was to replicate the naturalism and encourage the "happy accidents" that are an intrinsic part of traditional filmmaking.

01 Wildebeests, elephants, and zebras assemble at Pride Rock (*Concept artwork*)

"YOU HAVE STUDIED CINEMATOGRAPHY FOR A LONG TIME, AND THEN YOU END UP BEING KNOWN FOR THE ACCIDENTAL SHOT THAT WAS MUCH COOLER THAN THE PLANNED SHOT!"

The Lion King – The Official Movie Special: **This film has been produced using revolutionary virtual reality techniques; what was the thinking behind bringing more traditional filmmakers like Director of Photography Caleb Deschanel and Production Designer James Chinlund into that VR space?**

Rob Legato: Instead of only getting people who have experience in these sorts of visual effects, the idea was to get somebody who has 40 years' experience making great images on-screen naturally, and then build a tool that wasn't daunting for them, so they could walk in, grab a camera, and say; "We'll move the light over here; put the camera down low."

All of a sudden, it's like they're comfortable doing what they've done for 40 years, except they don't have to rush to get in a van and get to the top of the hill before they lose the light. They can shoot it right [there and then] – and then look for an even better setup. If they want to do it again, they just do it again without people coming down and saying they have to get out of there by five o'clock so they can make the other location. It has the benefit of all those things. It's like the Rosetta Stone for digital filmaking, a translation of what they already know traditionally in analog filmmaking: taking every skill you've ever had and applying it to a movie which is artificially created but looks perfectly real and natural.

How did you acclimatize Caleb Deschanel, James Chinlund, and the other departments to the VR space?

In this day and age, with, say, James and the art department, almost every set is designed on a computer anyway just as a normal part of production design. They no longer have to build study models or illustrations to realize their vision, they have a 3D set to explore from all angles and lighting conditions. So that part of that process is already in the VR zone.

But now there's a different form of a shared experience when we are all in VR at the same time with the ability to walk around and explore in life size. For example Jon or Caleb might say, "I think this shot's better over here," [to which James might reply,] "Well, if you're going to do that, maybe this tree should be here next to that stream." You start instantly applying the art form of the other talented collaborators with your own – and it happens automatically, without knowing it. It's just part of the discipline of live-action filmmaking. When the audience sees it, they shouldn't ever be aware of the process. To them it's just like a regular movie, only hopefully a very well done one.

It seems you're also incorporating the kinds of happy accidents you might get on a live-action shoot.

It's disturbing, because you have studied cinematography for a long time, and then you end up being known for the accidental shot that was much cooler than the planned shot ever was! If you're good, you tap into that; you accept that live input, and are able to admit that it was better than what you would have thought of.

You see some remarkable things in movies where somebody really liked the accident and then took advantage of it. There's a great story from *The Godfather*. Lenny Montanna, who played Luca Brasi, was not the greatest actor in the world (he had been a professional wrestler) – and when he went to do the scene with Marlon Brando, he was nervous and stammering, because ▶

02

ROB LEGATO
Selected Credits

FILMS
The Jungle Book, 2016
The Wolf of Wall Street, 2013
Hugo, 2011
Shutter Island, 2010
The Good Shepherd, 2006
The Departed, 2006
Aviator, 2005
Bad Boys II, 2003
Harry Potter and the Sorcerer's Stone, 2001
What Lies Beneath, 2000
Titanic, 1997
Apollo 13, 1994
Interview with the Vampire, 1992

TV
Star Trek: Deep Space Nine, 1993
Star Trek: The Next Generation, 1987-1988

03

02 A herd of elephants approach Pride Rock from a nearby hill (*Concept artwork*)

03 Watched over by Zazu, young Simba and Nala explore the Pride Lands (*Rendered film frame*)

"THE CREW WERE ABLE TO WALK INTO THE SAME ENVIRONMENT, EXPERIENCE THE SAME THINGS, AND THEN RIFF OFF ON EACH OTHER."

04

it was Marlon Brando! Francis Ford Coppola looked at that and decided to film him practicing his speech, so that when he goes and sees the Godfather, it looks like he's tongue-tied and so nervous he can barely get through his speech. He took what was once an intimidated non-actor and turned it into a great character moment. A brilliant piece of direction: he took advantage of something that was a negative and turned it into much more of a positive.

Francis being Francis, he would of course take advantage of anything that's great no matter where it came from, and make an enduring classic as a result. That's what we're trying to do here: let an accident happen, then take advantage of it.

Is the initial process on this film similar to the one you had on *The Jungle Book*?

It's the same as *The Jungle Book*. There's a storyboard/story department that fleshes it out – almost like the scriptwriting portion, where you see the script come to life and then alter the script to emphasize the beats. Then, once we get it on the VR stage it has already been visually vetted to some degree. Once you're in the VR environment, it's so much easier to create a moving shot or frame that really couldn't be explored that well in storyboard form. The idea might originally be there, but now it is fully explored from all angles and alternate blocking.

05

It is primarily what we did on *The Jungle Book*, except this time it was so much more immersive and much more collaborative. The crew was able to walk into the same environment with the other collaborators, experience the same things, and then riff off on each other what they each liked and wanted to take advantage of. Somebody like James could definitely benefit from Caleb's experience, and Caleb could definitely benefit from James being there while he was location scouting. It invites a discussion that you would otherwise never have. Hopefully the end result is much more cinematic, and will feel more like a movie that we're used to seeing.

How is lighting a scene in VR different to how you would do it on a regular movie set?

You essentially start with where you want the sun to be. Sometimes in a live-action film the sun can't be where you ideally want it. There might be a mountain in the way and a portion of the scene would be completely in shadow. What you would normally do is go find another, perhaps less production-friendly location to play a portion of the scene to cheat the reverses. You create the perfect location as a result on-screen but have hampered the production in the process or just have to live with compromised light. In our case, you would simply drop the light wherever it is needed regardless of the physical limitations. Visually, it looks just as authentic. If you know what you're doing, then you know how to cheat to create what looks like the ideal location every time.

How do you communicate within the VR space?

Because you're in the same space, like we are now, you just talk and say, "Come over and take a look at this." In VR you could be literally 20 miles away, and because you can't easily find the other person – even though in real life they're standing right next to you – Ben Grossmann and his team at Magnopus designed these tools with a little menu where you say, "Go to Caleb," and press a button, and you zip right over. It could be 20 miles away, and you go to exactly the same spot he is. It makes it easy to communicate, because you can do it verbally, and then you can see what he's seeing.

Once there you can instantly put your particular angle up on a big virtual screen for all to see and comment on. So the communication becomes so much better even than any of our live-action scouting experiences. On live-action location, at best you are crowded around the tiny screen of your phone, to try and describe your particular vision. Much less of a shared experience and certainly much less of putting your phone in the place of a real camera on crane or helicopter.

How do you populate these VR sets with the animals?

While some scenes will always need to be pre-animated, some chess piece stand-ins help previsualize the blocking and populate the shot in the scouting phase. While a chess piece can be very pliable and instantly moved and adjusted to block out a scene easily, it still needs to get properly animated to get the nuance of a performance before we could put a camera on it and rehearse the scene visually.

Phase one animation or chess piece blocking may not be very beautiful-looking – although it will be of course when Andy Jones and his team get a hold of it – but at least the first 15 questions are answered, like: Where do you start? When do you stop? How ▶

04 Timon, Pumbaa, and Simba cross a tree trunk bridge, echoing the classic 1994 movie (*Rendered film frame*)

05 Mufasa and young Simba walk around the Pride Lands – with every detail based on reference material gathered by the filmmakers (*Concept artwork*)

"THE UNIQUE POWER OF THIS STORY IS SO RICH, IT TRULY SHINES ONCE AGAIN WHEN EXPLORED THROUGH A BRAND-NEW LENS."

06 The magnificent waterfall centerpiece of the Cloud Forest (*Concept artwork*)

07 From the vantage point of Pride Rock, Mufasa shows his son the kingdom (*Rendered film frame*)

▶ close are you to your other actor? Are you behind the tree? In front of the tree? Are you walking uphill? Are you walking around the rock? Somebody has to answer all these things initially before you can even start rough animation. In VR you can answer them in real time in the real virtual location with a real virtual camera and have a much further evolved scene before it even gets to phase one animation. Phase two animation is brought back to stage to shoot all the angles of the scene while still having the freedom to visualize the scene from every vantage point.

That's all real time, and you want that real time feedback because you want to be able to change your mind, try things, see it four different ways before you settle on the one and say, "Now fine tune animate that." Then, when you bring it back to the stage and finally photograph the scene it is really the performance choices you wanted.

It's like writing the script visually. Each step gets you closer to the final because you see it fleshed out at every phase. By the time the audience sees it, it might have gone through 20 sophisticated revisions.

Do the character animations start from voice performances or vice versa?

It's a little bit of both. The preferred method is to get the naturalistic performance first and then animate and make decisions based on that, but it's almost like a chicken and egg thing. Sometimes you need to see something rough for the actors to then say, "Maybe we should play the scene this way," and that influences the script and the performance. So there's a bit of a dance between those that Jon has to balance out.

It definitely comes to life when the actors inhabit the character, and then the animators bounce off of that. Then the camera bounces off of that, and direction of the scene bounces... You really need all of it together.

What was the idea behind the black box theater?

The idea with the black box theater was to basically un-inhibit the actors. They could walk around, ad-lib, improv, spark off each other, and then the performances that come from that are

another iteration of the script. Jon's an actor, so he really likes that, because then he gets to interact with them.

We photograph the live performers with multiple cameras so the animators can see the intent of the actor. It's not a direct translation, because the actors aren't animals, but when they pause, look, stop, and you see them thinking, you know that that's the subtext that is driving the scene.

It's much more informed than just voices only. Disembodied voices reading off of a piece of paper is way different than interacting in a scene and bouncing ideas off of each other – and if one actor makes a mistake and the other actor doesn't break scene and covers it, maybe it creates something original and more interesting than what was scripted. Again, that's the happy accident that you can take advantage of, the same as you do all the time in a live-action movie.

With the 1994 *The Lion King* being such an iconic film, do you feel you have a lot to live up to?
It's a magnificent body of work, so that part is a little daunting.

We're doing our own take on it, as when they did the musical. The musical is not the animated movie. It's like getting a good novel and doing a really great interpretation of it – *The Godfather* or *Gone with the Wind*. A book's a book, and a movie's a movie. It's taking the essential core elements of the piece and translating it into another medium so it works as well while using the particular unique vocabulary of that new medium.

If you copy the animated *The Lion King* frame for frame, then you're going to end up with nothing since you didn't properly voice it in the strengths of the new live-action medium. You have to remind people what they saw, but you really can't copy it directly. What was once wonderful in a cartoon animated style simply would fall flat depicted in live action. While every once in a while, we do tip our cap to the animated set-up for a fun homage, we pretty much have to say this is a new unique piece of work based on our interpretation of the core material. You owe much more to the audience than simply remaking what came before us. The unique power of this story is so rich, it truly shines once again when explored through a brand-new lens.

DISNEY LIBRARY

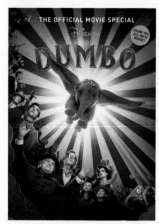

DISNEY *DUMBO*
THE OFFICIAL MOVIE SPECIAL

DISNEY•PIXAR *TOY STORY 4*
THE OFFICIAL MOVIE SPECIAL

DISNEY *THE LION KING*
THE OFFICIAL MOVIE SPECIAL

DISNEY *FROZEN 2*
THE OFFICIAL MOVIE SPECIAL
(OCTOBER 2019)

MARVEL LIBRARY

X-MEN
THE DARK PHOENIX SAGA (MAY '20)

NOVELS
- **ANT-MAN** NATURAL ENEMY
- **AVENGERS** EVERYBODY WANTS TO RULE THE WORLD
- **AVENGERS** INFINITY (NOV '19)
- **BLACK PANTHER** WHO IS THE BLACK PANTHER?
- **CAPTAIN AMERICA** DARK DESIGNS (OCT '19)
- **CAPTAIN MARVEL** LIBERATION RUN (OCT '19)
- **CIVIL WAR**
- **DEADPOOL** PAWS
- **SPIDER-MAN** FOREVER YOUNG
- **SPIDER-MAN** HOSTILE TAKEOVER
- **SPIDER-MAN** KRAVEN'S LAST HUNT
- **THANOS** DEATH SENTENCE
- **VENOM** LETHAL PROTECTOR
- **X-MEN** DAYS OF FUTURE PAST

MARVEL STUDIOS:
THE FIRST TEN YEARS

MOVIE SPECIALS
- **MARVEL STUDIOS' *ANT MAN & THE WASP***
- **MARVEL STUDIOS' *AVENGERS: ENDGAME***
- **MARVEL STUDIOS' *AVENGERS: INFINITY WAR***
- **MARVEL STUDIOS' *BLACK PANTHER* (COMPANION)**
- **MARVEL STUDIOS' *BLACK PANTHER* (SPECIAL)**
- **MARVEL STUDIOS' *CAPTAIN MARVEL***
- **MARVEL STUDIOS' *SPIDER-MAN: FAR FROM HOME***
- **MARVEL STUDIOS: THE FIRST TEN YEARS**
- **MARVEL STUDIOS' *THOR: RAGNAROK***
- **SPIDER-MAN: INTO THE SPIDERVERSE**

ARTBOOKS
- **MARVEL'S *SPIDER-MAN* THE ART OF THE GAME**
- **MARVEL: *CONQUEST OF CHAMPIONS* THE ART OF THE BATTLEREALM**
- **SPIDER-MAN: INTO THE SPIDERVERSE**
- **THE ART OF IRON MAN** 10TH ANNIVERSARY EDITION

STAR WARS LIBRARY

- **ROGUE ONE: A STAR WARS STORY** THE OFFICIAL COLLECTOR'S EDITION
- **ROGUE ONE: A STAR WARS STORY** THE OFFICIAL MISSION DEBRIEF
- **STAR WARS: THE LAST JEDI** THE OFFICIAL COLLECTOR'S EDITION
- **STAR WARS: THE LAST JEDI** THE OFFICIAL MOVIE COMPANION
- **STAR WARS: THE LAST JEDI** THE ULTIMATE GUIDE

- **SOLO: A STAR WARS STORY** THE OFFICIAL COLLECTOR'S EDITION
- **SOLO: A STAR WARS STORY** THE ULTIMATE GUIDE
- **THE BEST OF STAR WARS INSIDER** VOLUME 1
- **THE BEST OF STAR WARS INSIDER** VOLUME 2
- **THE BEST OF STAR WARS INSIDER** VOLUME 3
- **THE BEST OF STAR WARS INSIDER** VOLUME 4
- **STAR WARS: LORDS OF THE SITH**

- **STAR WARS: HEROES OF THE FORCE**
- **STAR WARS: ICONS OF THE GALAXY**
- **STAR WARS: THE SAGA BEGINS**
- **STAR WARS THE ORIGINAL TRILOGY**
- **STAR WARS: ROGUES, SCOUNDRELS AND BOUNTY HUNTERS (SEPTEMBER 2019)**
- **STAR WARS CREATURES, ALIENS, AND DROIDS**
- **STAR WARS: THE RISE OF SKYWALKER** THE OFFICIAL COLLECTOR'S EDITION (DEC 2019)

STAR WARS
THE SAGA BEGINS

STAR WARS:
THE RISE OF SKYWALKER
(DECEMBER 2019)

AVAILABLE AT ALL GOOD BOOKSTORES AND ONLINE

TITAN-COMICS.COM | TITANBOOKS.COM